# TEACHING KIT

A complete curriculum teaching kit is available to accompany this book. The curriculum is titled *How to Speak Your Spouse's Language* or *Are Men Really from Pluto and Women from Saturn?* It is possible to teach the content of the resource in marriage seminars, Sunday School classes, retreats, small groups, etc. The kit contains the structure, outline, time sequence and learning activities, as well as many transparency patterns that allow you to make professional-quality transparencies to use as you teach.

For information on ordering this unique teaching kit, either call Christian Marriage Enrichment at

**1 - 8 0 0 - 8 7 5 - 7 5 6 0**

or write to

**P.O. BOX 2468, ORANGE, CA 92859-0468.**

# COMMUNICATION
## KEY TO YOUR MARRIAGE

*A*

*Practical Guide*

*to Creating a*

*Happy,*

*Fulfilling*

*Relationship*

# H. NORMAN WRIGHT
*Your Trusted Marriage and Family Counselor*

**Regal**

**A Division of Gospel Light**
**Ventura, California, U.S.A.**

Published by Regal Books
A Division of Gospel Light
Ventura, California, U.S.A.
Printed in the U.S.A.

Regal Books is a ministry of Gospel Light, an evangelical Christian publisher dedicated to serving the local church. We believe God's vision for Gospel Light is to provide church leaders with biblical, user-friendly materials that will help them evangelize, disciple and minister to children, youth and families.

It is our prayer that this Regal book will help you discover biblical truth for your own life and help you meet the needs of others. May God richly bless you.

For a free catalog of resources from Regal Books/Gospel Light, please call your Christian supplier or contact us at 1-800-4-GOSPEL or www.regalbooks.com.

Cover Design by Mike Berger at David Riley & Associates
Interior Design by Rob Williams
Edited by Deena Davis; Fritz Ridenour, editor of original edition

**Library of Congress Cataloging-in-Publication Data**

Wright, H. Norman.
    Communication: key to your marriage / H. Norman Wright.—[Rev. ed.].
        p. cm.
    Included bibliographical references.
ISBN 0-8307-2533-4
    1. Communication in marriage—United States. 2. Marriage—Religious aspects—Christianity. I. Title.

HQ536.W68 2000
248.8'44
[21]                                                                00-036605

1  2  3  4  5  6  7  8  9  10  11  12  13  14  15  /  07  06  05  04  03  02  01  00

Rights for publishing this book in other languages are contracted by Gospel Literature International (GLINT). GLINT also provides technical help for the adaptation, translation and publishing of Bible study resources and books in scores of languages worldwide. For further information, contact GLINT, P.O. Box 4060, Ontario, CA 91761-1003, U.S.A. You may also send e-mail to Glintint@aol.com, or visit their website at www.glint.org.

# CONTENTS

# MARRIAGE
# EXPECTATIONS

### CHAPTER ONE

Why did you marry? Can you remember back to that time when your life was filled with dreams, expectations and hopes for the future? What part did marriage play in those dreams and hopes? What did you expect from marriage? Perhaps your answer includes one or more of the following:

- I wanted to share my life experiences with someone.
- I wanted someone to help make me happy.
- I wanted to spend my life with someone I loved and with someone who loved me.
- I wanted to fulfill what I lacked in my own home.
- I wanted to be faithful to God and love someone He wanted me to love.
- I didn't want to end up alone, especially when I was older. Marriage was that security.

All of these are fringe benefits of marriage, but none is strong enough to stand as its foundation.

Many people are propelled toward marriage without really understanding all they are committing themselves to for the rest of their lives. That's why couples experience surprises and upsets throughout the duration of their marriage.

Various writers have given definitions of "Christian marriage." Wayne Oates says: "Marriage is a covenant of responsible love, a fellowship of repentance and forgiveness."

David Augsburger defines marriage by first asking, "Is marriage a private action of two persons in love, or a public act of two pledging a contract?" Then he goes on to say, "Neither. It is something other. Very much other!"

> Basically the Christian view of marriage is not that it is primarily or even essentially a binding legal and social contract. The Christian understands marriage as a covenant made under God and in the presence of fellow members of the Christian family. Such a pledge endures, not because the force of law or the fear of its sanctions, but because an unconditional covenant has been made. A covenant more solemn, more binding, more permanent than any legal contract.[1]

Some psychologists, marriage counselors and ministers have suggested that marriage is a contract, and many people are quick to agree. But is this really true?

In every contract there are certain conditional clauses. A contract between two parties, whether they are companies or individuals, involves the responsibility of both parties to carry out their part of the bargain. These are conditional clauses—*if clauses* (if you do this, the other person must do this). There are no conditional clauses in the marriage relationship and the marriage ceremony. The marriage ceremony vows do not state,

"If the husband loves his wife, then the wife continues in the contract." Or, "If the wife is submissive to her husband, then the husband carries out the contract." Marriage is an unconditional commitment into which two people enter.

In most contracts there are *escape clauses*. An escape clause says that if the party of the first part does not carry out his responsibilities, then the party of the second part is absolved. If one person does not live up to his or her part of the bargain, the second person can get out of the contract. In marriage, there is no escape clause.

Then if marriage is not a contract, what is it? It is an unconditional commitment into which a man and woman enter *for life*.

## What Makes Marriage Last

Commitment means many things to different people. For some, the strength of their commitment varies with how they feel emotionally or physically. The word "commit" is a verb that means to do or to perform. It is not based primarily on feelings. It is a binding pledge or promise. It is a private pledge you also make publicly. It is a pledge carried out to completion, no matter the roadblocks. It is a total giving of one's self to another person. Yes, it is risky, but it makes life fulfilling.

Commitment requires you to give up the childish dream of being unconditionally accepted by your partner and expecting that partner to fulfill all your needs and make up for all your childhood disappointments. It means that you expect to be disappointed by your partner at times and that you learn to accept this and not use it as a reason to pull the plug.[2]

Perhaps a better way to describe commitment is to compare it to bungee jumping. If you've ever taken the plunge, you know

Commitment is more than maintaining; it is more than continuing to stick it out with a poor choice of a spouse. Commitment is investing— working to make the relationship grow.

that when you take that step off the platform, you are committed to follow through. There's no more time to think it over or change your mind. There's no turning back.

A friend of mine shared with me what has made his marriage last. He said, "Norm, we each had a commitment to each other and to the marriage. When our commitment to each other was low, it was the commitment to the marriage that kept us together."

To some people, commitment to another person until death seems idealistic. They are committed when it suits them and they're not inconvenienced. But when certain problems occur, commitment is no longer valid.

Commitment is more than maintaining; it is more than continuing to stick it out and suffer with a poor choice of a spouse. Commitment is investing—working to make the relationship grow. It's not about just accepting and tolerating a spouse's negative and destructive patterns of relating; it means working toward change. It means sticking to someone regardless of circumstances. Listen to one wife's story.

In 1988, I was diagnosed with Epstein-Barr virus (chronic fatigue syndrome). It really changed my life, which had been filled with excitement and vibrancy. My husband, Kelly, has stood with me and become my protector through these years of adjustment. He has taken care of our family when my strength would not allow me. He has held my hand through depression, including ten days in the hospital. He has insisted I get needed rest, even if it put more of a burden on him. He has paid the price of any hopeful cure we have found, no matter the cost. He has been more than a husband, he has been my best friend—a friend that has stayed closer than any family member. He was my knight in shining armor when I met him and he has proven to be so throughout our 14 ½ years of marriage. I sometimes tell him that he has been my salvation, because I don't know that I would still be going on if it weren't for his strength. I don't know that I would still walk with the Lord if it were not for his encouragement. Knowing him has been the greatest experience in my life.

## When Life Changes

There will be ups and downs throughout the life of a marriage. There will be massive changes—some predictable and others intrusive—that hold the potential for growth as well as risk. Many marriages die because too many people choose to ignore the inescapable fact that relationships and people change.

A wife shared the following about dealing with the risk as well as the potential for growth:

Since we have been married fifty years, you can just imagine how much change we have gone through: three wars, eleven presidents, five recessions, going from the Model-A [automobile] to the moon, from country roads to the information superhighway. While these changes around us have been great, the personal changes that God has enacted within us through each other have been even greater. Although we often couldn't see how God was working in our lives at that time, we look back now and realize that our marriage has been a school of character development. God has used my husband in my life and He's used me in his life to make us more like Christ. So what are the lessons we've learned about how God uses marriage to change us? There are many. Through fifty years of marriage we've learned that differences develop us, that crises cultivate us and that ministry melts us together.

First, God has used our differences to help us grow. There have been many, many crises that God has used to develop us and to grow us. The first one was the big one—the crisis of being separated as soon as we got married. Ours was a wartime romance. We met at church, dated two months and got married after three weeks of engagement; and just after two months of marriage, we didn't see each other for the next two years when Jimmy was shipped to the South Pacific during World War II. When he returned, we were total strangers, but we were married to each other!

How would you have handled that situation?

I think the following comments by a wife illustrate the life-long expression of love and commitment.

Real life death scenes aren't like the movies. My husband, too tall for a regulation bed, lay with his feet sticking out of the covers. I stood clinging to his toes as though that would save his life. I clung so that if I failed to save him from falling off the cliff of the present, of the here and now, we'd go together. That's how it was in the nether-world of the intensive care unit. . . .

It seemed that the entire world had turned into night. Cold and black. No place you'd volunteer to enter. Doctors tried to be kind. Their eyes said, "This is out of our hands. There's nothing more we can do."

A nurse with a soft Jamaican lilt [to her voice] placed a pink blanket over my shoulders. Someone whispered, "It's just a matter of minutes."

Just a matter of minutes to tell each other anything we had ever forgotten to say. Just a few minutes to take an accounting of our days together. Had we loved well enough?[3]

## God's Perspective of Marriage

What does God's Word say about marriage? Genesis 2:18-25 (*RSV*) teaches that marriage was God's idea and that He had several divine purposes in mind.

Then the LORD God said, "It is not good that the man should be alone; I will make him a helper fit for him." So out of the ground the LORD God formed every beast of the field and every bird of the air, and brought them to the man to see what he would call them; and what-ever the man called every living creature, that was its name. The man gave names to all cattle, and to the birds of the air, and to every beast of the field; but for the man there was not found a helper fit for him. So the LORD God caused a deep sleep to fall upon the man, and while he slept took one of his ribs and closed up its place with flesh; and the rib which the LORD God had taken from the man he made into a woman and brought her to the man. Then the man said, "This at last is bone of my bones and flesh of my flesh; she shall be called Woman, because she was taken out of Man." Therefore a man leaves his father and his mother and cleaves to his wife, and they become one flesh. And the man and his wife were both naked, and were not ashamed.

## Companionship

God created marriage for *companionship*. As John Milton observed, "Loneliness was the first thing God's eye named not good." Loneliness and isolation are contradictions to the purpose in God's creative act. God made man to live with others, and the first other was woman.

When God said it wasn't good for man to be alone, He meant that in every way it wasn't good.

It wasn't good physically; there was no partner.

It wasn't good emotionally; there was no one to share with.

It wasn't good spiritually.

## Completeness

God also created marriage for *completeness*. The woman was to be "a helper fit for him" (v. 18). The woman assists man in making his life (and hers) complete. She fills up the empty places. She shares his life with him and draws him out of himself into a wider area of contact through the involvement they have with one another. She is one who can enter into responsible companionship. The partners in a marriage relationship are actually fulfilling God's purpose of completeness, or wholeness, in life.

## Communication

The companionship and completeness God intended for marriage grow out of *communication* as two people share each day the meaning of their lives. As Dwight Small says, "The heart of marriage is its communication system. . . . But no couple begins marriage with highly developed communication. It is not something they bring into marriage ready, but something to be continually cultivated through all the experiences of their shared life."[4] Satisfying companionship and a sense of completeness develop as husband and wife learn to communicate with openness and understanding. Andre M. Aurois is credited with saying that a happy marriage is a long conversation that always seems too short. What about it? How do you relate to that statement?

When you exchanged your wedding vows, the words "leave" and "cleave" became part of your life. Did you understand these words? To leave means to sever one relationship before establishing another. This does not mean that you disregard your parents. Rather, it requires that you break your tie to them and assume responsibility for your spouse.

To cleave means to weld together. When a man cleaves to his wife, they become one flesh. This term is a beautiful capsule description of the oneness, completeness and permanence that God intended in the marriage relationship. It suggests a unique oneness—a total commitment to intimacy in all of life together, symbolized by the sexual union.

Years ago I heard a choice description of the coming together involved in cleaving. If you hold a lump of dark green clay in one hand and a lump of light green clay in the other hand, you can clearly identify the two different shades of color. However, when you mold the two lumps together, at first glance you see just one lump of green clay. When you inspect the lump closely you see the distinct and separate lines of dark and light green clay.

This is a picture of your marriage relationship. The two of you are blended together so that you appear as one, yet each of you retains your distinct identity and personality. But now you have a marriage personality that exists in the two of you.

A Christian marriage involves more than the blending of two people. It also includes a third person—Jesus Christ—who gives meaning, guidance and direction to the relationship. When He presides in a marriage, then and only then is it a Christian marriage.

Since your wedding, how have you handled leaving your parents? How have you become one flesh with your spouse, coming together and yet retaining who you are as individuals? Why not talk about it?

## What's Your Plan?

Think back to the time before you were married.

1. What did you think marriage would be like? Did it turn out the way you expected?
2. Did you and your spouse have different expectations for marriage? How did you discover the differences? Have you talked directly about these differences?
3. I expected marriage to change my lifestyle by . . .

4. I believe my mate expected me to be . . .

5. I expected my mate to be more . . .

*Notes*

1. David Augsburger, *Cherishable: Love and Marriage* (Scottdale, Penn.: Herald Press, 1971), p. 16.

2. Rebecca Cutter, *When Opposites Attract* (New York: Dutton, 1994), p. 189, adapted.

3. Barbara Ascher, "Above All, Love," *Redbook* (February 1992), n.p.

4. Dwight Harvey Small, *After You've Said "I Do"* (Grand Rapids, Mich.: Fleming H. Revell, 1968), pp. 11, 16.

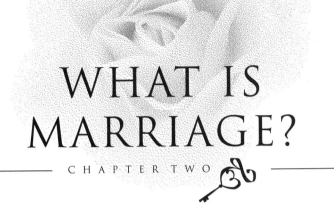

# WHAT IS MARRIAGE?

CHAPTER TWO

If someone asked you the question "Just what *is* marriage, anyway?" how would you answer that question? Let's consider a number of the factors that make marriage what it is:

Marriage is a gift.

Marriage is an opportunity to learn how to love.

Marriage is a journey in which we as travelers face many choices and are responsible for those choices.

Marriage is built upon a commitment to communicate. We have to learn to speak our partners' language.

Marriage is often influenced, more than we realize, by unresolved issues from our past.

Marriage is a call to servanthood.

Marriage is a call to friendship.

Marriage is a call to suffering.

Marriage is a refining process. It is an opportunity to be refined by God into the people He wants us to be.

Marriage is not an event but a way of life.

Marriage involves intimacy in all areas. This intimacy must reach into the spiritual, the intellectual, the social, the emotional and the physical.

In this chapter we'll consider four of these components—marriage as a gift, as a call to servanthood, as an intimate relationship and a refining process. Think about each of these components as you reflect on your own marriage relationship. What you believe about marriage and what you expect out of your marriage have a direct effect on communication between you and your spouse.

## Marriage Is a Gift

What do you think of the statement that you may be the finest gift your spouse has ever received and that your spouse may be the finest gift you have ever received?

A gift is an item selected with care and consideration. Its purpose is to bring delight and fulfillment to another; it is an expression of deep feeling on the part of the giver. Think of the care and effort you put into selecting a gift. You wonder what the recipient would enjoy—what would bring delight, happiness or cheer. You want to give something that would show the person the extent of your feeling and how much the person means to you.

Because you want this gift to be special and meaningful, you begin the search through various stores and shops, considering and rejecting several items until the right one beckons and you make the selection. You invest time wrapping the gift. You think of how best to present it to the person so that his or her delight and pleasure are heightened.

There is excitement and challenge involved in selecting and presenting a special gift. Not only have you given the object, you have also given your time and energy. The gifts that are often appreciated the most are not the most expensive ones but are the ones that reflect the investment of the giver in considering the desires and wants of the other person.

*You are a gift to your spouse.* When you consider the fact that you are a gift, how might you live so that your spouse feels that he or she has been given a special gift? How can you, as a gift, be used in the life of your spouse to lift his or her spirits and outlook on life?

On the receiving end of the gift, how do you react when you receive a special gift that brings you delight? Think of your childhood or earlier years. Can you remember the most exciting or special gift you ever received? Can you remember your thoughts and feelings as you received that gift? How did you treat that gift? Did you take special care of it and protect it from harm? Perhaps you gave the gift a special place of prominence and were carefully possessive of it.

If your spouse is a special gift to you, how do you treat this precious gift? Are you careful to give your spouse the finest care, attention, protection and a place of prominence in your life?

Does your partner feel as though he or she really is a gift to you?

We give a gift as an expression of our love and as an act of grace. We do not give it based on whether the recipient deserves it or not.

## What Do You Think?

1. What is the best tangible gift your spouse has ever given you?
2. What is the best intangible gift your spouse has ever given you?
3. What is the gift you would like to give to your spouse?
4. What would your spouse appreciate?

## Marriage Is Servanthood

Marriage is a call to servanthood. This is not a very popular concept and not high on the list of priorities for most marriages. We would much rather be served than serve. Take a look at what Scripture gives us as a guideline for Christian marriage:

> If you've gotten anything at all out of following Christ, if his love has made any difference in your life, if being in a community of the Spirit means anything to you, if you have a heart, if you *care*—then do me a favor: Agree with each other, love each other, be deep-spirited friends. Don't push your way to the front; don't sweet-talk your way to the top. Put yourself aside, and help others get ahead. Don't be obsessed with getting your own advantage. Forget yourselves long enough to lend a helping hand.

Think of yourselves the way Christ Jesus thought of himself. He had equal status with God but didn't think so much of himself that he had to cling to the advantages of that status no matter what. Not at all. When the time came, he set aside the privileges of deity and took on the status of a slave, became *human!* Having become human, he stayed human. It was an incredibly humbling process. He didn't claim special privileges. Instead, he lived a selfless, obedient life and then died a selfless, obedient death—and the worst kind of death at that: a crucifixion (Phil. 2:1-8, *THE MESSAGE*).

Jesus voluntarily submitted to becoming a bond servant. He looked out for our interests rather than His own. In the same way, the apostle Paul tells us to "be subject to one another in the fear of Christ" (Eph. 5:21).

Notice one important point: We must never *demand* that our partner be our servant or live up to the clear teachings of Scripture. If we feel that we have to demand it or even mention it, then we become more concerned with meeting our own needs than with being a servant. If a man has to demand that his wife view him as the head of the family, then—to put it bluntly—he has lost the headship! Verses 22-25 of Ephesians 5 say that for a man to be the head he must love his wife as Christ loved the Church and gave Himself for her. This means sacrificial love—servanthood.

### Who Submits to Whom?

The Greek word translated "submit" in Ephesians 5:21 (*NIV*) is *hupotasso*. It is also translated "subject" and is used several times in the New Testament. The active form of this verb is a military term.

It signifies an externally imposed submission based upon some-one's rank or position, just as a private or sergeant would submit to a captain or lieutenant. In Scripture, the word "hupotasso" emphasizes the rule of Jesus Christ, as found in Romans 8:20 when speaking of creation's being subject to Christ. Again, in 1 Corinthians 15:27, on three occasions God is said to have put all things under Jesus' feet, making them subject to Him. This is "hupotasso" in the active voice.

However, the word has another form—the middle, or passive, voice. Here, subjection is not something arbitrarily done to you; it is something you do voluntarily to yourself. In the various marriage texts, such as those found in Ephesians 5, Colossians 3, Titus 2, and 1 Peter 3, the word "hupotasso" is in the middle, or passive, voice. The submission you are called to in marriage is never anything *externally* imposed; it is a definite act on your part that comes from *inside* you. And it is a mutual submission; it involves both of you!

A great deal has been said in recent years about the husband-wife relationship as described in Scripture. With the feminist movement demanding that women be treated as equals, Bible scholars have struggled with the true meaning of passages such as Ephesians 5. Some have incorrectly interpreted the word "sub-mit" in the military sense of the word, proclaiming absolute headship of the husband. Others have swung the other way, say-ing that husbands and wives are equal, and the only kind of bib-lical marriage is one of equal partnership. As often happens, we struggle with one of many paradoxes in Scripture.

I think perhaps David Small best describes the biblical roles of husbands and wives in his book *Marriage as Equal Partnership*:

It is good that husband-wife equality is a prominent concern in our time. We are wholeheartedly in favor of extending that equality to every facet of daily living. But there is one thing we must remember. Equality is one principle among others; it doesn't stand alone and unqualified as though it were the only word of God to us. It is only part of the divine equation. It is entirely true; it is not the entire truth. And what humanly seems contradictory to us may be a divine paradox. Thus, in Ephesians 5:21-33 it becomes obvious that husbands and wives are equal in every respect save one—authority and responsibility.

As we've begun to see, this inequality in authority-responsibility is mitigated inasmuch as the husband carries this as his own peculiar burden before the Lord. It is not to be envied, only supported prayerfully. What truly does alleviate all wifely fear is the call to mutual love and Christlike service at the heart of this paradoxical relationship. Its beauty, symmetry, and fairness unfold as we place ourselves within these special conditions under which biblical marriage functions.

Headship is not at all a husband's becoming a master, boss, tyrant, authoritarian—the dominant coercive force. Neither does it imply control or restriction, his being assertive and hers being suppressed. It cannot mean he assumes any prerogatives of greater virtue, intelligence, or ability. It does not mean that he is active and she passive, he the voice and she the silent partner. Nor does it mean that he is the tribal chief, the family manager, the one who has superior rights or privileges. He is not the decision-maker, problem-solver, goal-setter, or director of everyone else in the family's life. Rather he is primarily responsible for their common advance toward freedom and fellowship—creating a partnership of equals under one responsible head.

A truly loving husband will regard his wife as a completely equal partner in everything that concerns their life together. He will assert his headship to see that this equal partnership is kept inviolable. Hers is to be an equal contribution in areas, say, of decision-making, conflict-resolution, emerging family developmental planning, and daily family management. Whether it concerns finances or child discipline or social life—whatever it may be, she is an equal partner. Loving headship affirms, defers, shares; it encourages and stimulates. Loving headship delights to delegate without demanding. Yet, throughout the equalitarian process, the husband knows all the while that he bears the responsibility before God for the healthful maintenance of the marriage.[1]

To put it simply, a servant's role is to make sure that the other person's needs are met. In a husband-wife relationship, being a servant is an act of love, a gift to the other person. It is not something to be demanded. It is an act of strength and not of weakness. It is a positive action chosen to show your love to each another. Hence, the apostle Paul also said, "Be subject to one another" (Eph. 5:21), not limiting the role of servanthood to the wife.

A servant may also be called an *enabler*. Here it has nothing to do with dysfunction; it is a positive term. The word "enable" means to make better. As an enabler we are to make life easier for our spouse instead of placing restrictive demands upon him or her. An enabler does not make more work for the partner, nor does the enabler hinder the other from becoming all he or she was designed to become.

A servant is also one who *edifies* or builds up the other person. The English word "edify" is derived from the Latin word *aedes,* meaning "hearth" or "fireplace." The hearth was the center of activity in ancient times. It was the only place of warmth and light in the home and the place where the daily bread was prepared. It was also the place where people were drawn together.

The concept of edifying is often used in the New Testament to refer to building up another person. Three examples of edifying are expressed in the verses below: (1) personal encouragement, (2) inner strengthening and (3) the establishment of peace and harmony between individuals.

> So let's agree to use all our energy in getting along with each other. Help others with encouraging words; don't drag them down by finding fault (Rom. 14:19, *THE MESSAGE*).

> Let each one of us make it a practice to please (make happy) his neighbor for his

In a marriage relationship, being a servant is an act of love, a gift to the other person. It is not something to be demanded. It is an act of strength and not of weakness.

good and for his true welfare, to edify him [to strength-
en him and build him up spiritually] (Rom. 15:2, *AMP*).

Therefore encourage one another and build each other
up, just as in fact you are doing (1 Thess. 5:11, *NIV*).

Love builds up (1 Cor. 8:1, *NIV*).

To edify, then, means to cheer another person in life. You are
a one-person rooting section for your spouse; your encouragement can increase your spouse's feelings of self-worth, enhanc-
ing his or her capacity to love and to give in return.

## What Do You Think?

1. Give two examples of how your partner believes you
   respond as a servant.
2. How does your partner edify you?
3. How would your partner like you to edify him or her?
   If you are unsure, why not ask?

## Marriage Is an Intimate Relationship

Marriage is a way of life, a celebration of life. A wedding ends,
but a marriage progresses until the death of one of the partners.
The conclusion of the wedding marks the beginning of a marriage relationship, which is a call to intimacy. Intimacy is shared
identity, a "we" relationship. Its opposite is a marriage in which
the individuals are called married singles—each partner going
his own way. In shared intimacy there must be a level of honesty

that makes each partner vulnerable to the other. Intimacy is a multistringed musical instrument. The music from a viola comes not from one string but from a combination of different strings and finger positions.

We hear a great deal today about physical intimacy, often referring to nothing more than the physical act of two bodies copulating. However, the basis for true physical intimacy actually results from *emotional intimacy*.

Physical intimacy involves the marriage of emotions as well as bodies. Emotions give color to life. Emotional intimacy may elude many couples because one or both partners make no conscious effort to develop intimacy by lowering barriers and walls. Judson Swihart writes of the tragedy of a marriage lacking emotional intimacy:

> Some people are like medieval castles. Their high walls keep them safe from being hurt. They protect themselves emotionally by permitting no exchange of feelings with others. No one can enter. They are secure from attack. However, inspection of the occupant finds him or her lonely, rattling around his castle alone. The castle dweller is a self-made prisoner. He or she needs to feel loved by someone, but the walls are so high that it is difficult to reach out or for anyone else to reach in.2

Even if barriers are not an issue, a man's and a woman's emotions may be at different levels and intensities. A woman's priority may be emotional intimacy, whereas a man's priority may be physical intimacy. When a couple learns to share the emotional level and can understand and experience each other's feelings, they are well on their way to achieving true intimacy.

When a couple learns to share on the emotional level and can understand and experience each other's feelings, they are well on their way to achieving true intimacy.

By the way, do you really understand what intimacy means? The word "intimacy" is derived from the Latin word *intimus,* meaning "inmost." Intimacy suggests a very strong personal relationship, a special *emotional* closeness that includes understanding and being understood by someone who is very special. Intimacy has also been defined as "an affectionate bond, the strands of which are composed of mutual caring, responsibility, trust, open communication of feelings and sensations, as well as the nondefended interchange of information about significant emotional events."[3] Intimacy means taking the risk to be close to someone and allowing that someone to step inside your personal boundaries.

Intimacy requires vulnerability, but it also requires security. Openness can be scary, but the acceptance each partner offers in the midst of vulnerability provides a wonderful sense of security. Intimate couples can feel safe—fully exposed perhaps, yet fully accepted.

It is often assumed that intimacy automatically occurs between married partners. But I've seen far too many "strangers" get married. I've talked to many husbands and wives who feel isolated from each other and lonely, even after many years of marriage. I've heard statements like: "We share the same house, the same table and the same bed, but we might as well be strangers"; "We've lived together for 23 years and yet I don't know my spouse any better now than when we married"; "What really hurts is that we can spend a weekend together and I still feel lonely. I think I married someone who would have preferred being a hermit in some ways."

Intimacy is not automatic. Communication is the vehicle for creating and maintaining intimacy, and it is the means by which we know another person.

## Levels of Communication

Take a moment to evaluate the intimacy in your marriage relationship. Explore how you deal with intimacy as a couple by circling your responses to the following statements. Work through the exercise separately, then explain your responses to each other.

1. When it comes to conversational intimacy, the way I see our relationship is . . .

    a. We say a lot but reveal little of our real selves.
    b. We reveal our real selves, but we don't say very much.
    c. We say a lot and reveal a lot of our real selves.
    d. We say little and reveal little of our real selves.

2. When it comes to sharing with you what I'm really thinking, feeling, wanting or not wanting . . .

a. I keep my inner self well hidden.
b. I reveal as much as I feel safe to share.
c. I let it all hang out.

3. When it comes to sharing with me what you are really thinking, feeling, wanting or not wanting . . .

a. You seem to keep your inner self well hidden.
b. You seem to reveal as much as you feel safe to share.
c. You seem to let it all hang out.

4. Some ways I avoid intimacy when we are getting uncomfortably close are . . .

a. I laugh or crack a joke.
b. I shrug it off and act as if it doesn't matter.
c. I act confused—like I don't know what is going on.
d. I look angry so that you can't see into me too deeply.
e. I get angry or huffy, especially when I am feeling vulnerable.
f. I get overly talkative.
g. I get analytical—hiding behind a wall of intellectualizing.
h. I change the subject so I won't have to deal with it.
i. I act strong, together, above it all—especially when feeling vulnerable.

5. From the list above, some ways I see you avoid intimacy when we are getting uncomfortably close are . . .

6. The reason I avoid intimacy this way is . . .

7. The effect of avoiding intimacy in this way is . . .

8. In order to build intimacy in our relationship, I would now be willing to . . .[4]

There are five levels of conversation that correspond to degrees of intimacy in a marriage relationship. As you read about each level, pause to answer the two questions as they relate to your marriage.

*The first level* of conversation is limited to sharing facts, explanations or information. Conversations at this level are much like exchanging newspaper stories. While the information can be interesting, it is often considered small talk and really doesn't accomplish much in getting to know another person. The degree of intimacy at this conversation level is extremely shallow.

1. When does this type of conversation occur in your marriage?

2. Which of you tends to use this style of conversation more?

The second level of conversation centers on sharing the ideas and opinions of other people. Conversation at this level is a bit more interesting and yet discloses little of oneself. Practically no intimacy is achieved when discussion is limited to persons outside the relationship.

1. When does this type of conversation occur in your marriage?

2. Which of you tends to use this style of conversation more?

Conversation level three produces moderate intimacy. At this level, you are sharing your own ideas and opinions. You are disclosing some of your own thoughts and risking minor vulnerability, but you are still not revealing who you really are.

1. When does this type of conversation occur in your marriage?

2. Which of you tends to use this style of conversation more?

*Level four* involves a higher degree of intimacy in conversation. Now you are sharing personal preferences, beliefs, concerns and also some of your own personal experiences. One of the level-four questions my daughter often asked me when she was young was, "Daddy, what were you like when you were a little boy?" I was amazed at how much I began to recall and share about myself in response to her question.

1. When does this type of conversation occur in your marriage?

2. Which of you tends to use this style of conversation more?

*Level five* is the highest level of conversation and communication. Here you share your inner feelings and preferences, likes and dislikes. You share what is occurring in your inner life and you open up completely. You move beyond talking about events or beliefs or ideas or opinions to talking about how these ideas or events or people influence you and how they touch you emotionally and inwardly. At this level, emotional expression has moved from talking from the head to talking from the heart.

1. When does this type of conversation occur in your marriage?

2. Which of you tends to use this style of conversation most?

## Marriage Is a Refining Process

Our response to life's crises is the key issue. When troubles come, we may say, "God, this isn't what I wanted in my life; I didn't plan for this." But the trouble is there, regardless of our wishes. How will we respond to it?

A verse that has meant so much to me is one I ask couples in premarital counseling to build their marriage upon: "Consider it all joy, my brethren, when you encounter various trials, knowing that the testing [or trying] of your faith produces endurance" (Jas. 1:2,3). It's easy to read a passage like this and say, "Well, that's fine." It's another thing to put it into practice.

What does the word "consider" mean? It refers to an internal attitude of the heart or the mind that allows the trial or circumstance to affect us either adversely or beneficially. Another way James 1:2 might be translated is: Make up your mind to regard adversity as something to welcome or be glad about.

You have the power to decide what your attitude will be. You can approach a circumstance by saying, *It's terrible. Totally upsetting. This is the last thing I wanted for my life. Why did it have to happen now? Why me?*

The other way of considering the same difficulty is to say, *It's not what I wanted or expected, but it's here. How can I make the best of these difficult times?* Never deny the pain or the hurt you might have to go through. Instead ask, *What can I learn from this difficult time and how can it be used for God's glory?*

The verb tense used in the word "consider" indicates a decisive action. It's not an attitude of resignation—*Well, I guess I'll just give up. I'm stuck with this problem. That's the way life is.* Actually, the verb tense indicates that you will have to put forth some effort and go against your natural inclination to view trials as a negative force. You will have to say to yourself, *I think there is a better way of responding to this. Lord, I really want you to help me see it from a different perspective.* It will take a lot of work on your part, but it will shift your mind to a more constructive response.

God created us with the capacity and the freedom to determine how we will respond to the unexpected incidents life brings our way. You may honestly wish that a certain event had never occurred, but you can't change the fact that it has.

My wife, Joyce, and I had to learn to look to God in the midst of a seeming tragedy. We had two children: a daughter, Sheryl, and a son, Matthew. Our son never advanced beyond the cognitive level of a two-year-old. He was classified as profoundly retarded. And at the age of 22, he died.

We did not anticipate becoming the parents of a mentally retarded son. We married upon graduation from college, proceeded through seminary and graduate school training and went into a local church ministry. Several years later, Matthew was born.

As I look at my life, I know that I have been an impatient, selfish person in many ways. But because of Matthew I have had the opportunity to develop patience. When you wait a long time for a child to be able to reach out and handle an item, when you wait for three or four years for him to learn to walk, you develop patience. We had to learn to be sensitive to a person who could not verbally communicate his needs, hurts or wants. We had to decipher what he was trying to say; we had to try to interpret his nonverbal behavior.

Needless to say, Joyce and I grew and changed through this process. We experienced times of hurt, frustration and sorrow. But we rejoiced and learned to thank God for those tiny steps of progress most people would take for granted. The meaning of the name Matthew—"God's gift" or "gift from God"—became very real to us.

We might easily have chosen bitterness over our son's problem. We could have let it become a source of estrangement in our marriage, hindering our growth as individuals. But God enabled us to select a path of acceptance. We grew and matured—together. Not instantly, but over the course of several years. There have been steep places to overcome; but there have also been highlights and rich moments of reflection and delight. Matthew became the refining agent God used to change us.

My wife and I have discovered a great deal about the way God works in our lives. We realize that He prepared us years before Matthew's coming, though we hadn't realized the preparation was taking place. When I was in seminary I was required to write a thesis. Not knowing what to write about, I asked one of my professors to suggest a topic. She assigned me the title, "The Christian Education of the Mentally Retarded Child." I knew absolutely nothing on the subject, but I learned in a hurry. I read books, went to classes, observed training sessions in hospitals and homes and finally wrote the thesis. I rewrote it three times and my wife typed it three times before it was accepted.

Later on, my graduate studies in psychology required several hundred hours of internship in a school district. The district assigned me the task of testing mentally retarded children and placing them in their respective classes.

While serving as minister of education in a church for six years, I was asked by the church board to develop a Sunday School program for retarded children. My duties included developing the ministry and the curriculum and training the teachers.

Two years before Matthew was born, Joyce and I were talking one evening. One of us said, "Isn't it interesting that we have all this exposure to retarded children? We've been learning so much. Could it be that God is preparing us for something later on in our life?" That's all we said at the time, and I can't even remember which one of us said it. Within a year, Matthew was born. Eight months later his seizures began. The uncertainty we had felt over the rate of his progress was now a deep concern. When we learned the full truth, we began to see how the Lord had prepared us.

This is what He does for you. When you go through your difficult times, you will discover that He either has already prepared you for that difficulty or He will give you the resources you need at that time. This is a promise of Scripture.

Where does the call to suffering enter this whole process? Romans 8:16,17 says, "The Spirit Himself bears witness with our spirit that we are children of God, and if children, heirs also, heirs of God and fellow heirs with Christ, if indeed we suffer with Him in order that we may also be glorified with Him." As members of the Body of Christ, we suffer when one member suffers.

In the minor or major crises that will occur in your marriage, each of you will experience hurt. But a hurt shared, diminishes; hurt carried alone expands. Lewis B. Smedes describes marital suffering in this way:

Anybody's marriage is a harvest of suffering. Romantic lotus-eaters may tell you marriage was designed to be a pleasure dome for erotic spirits to frolic in self-fulfilling relations. But they play you false. Your marriage vow was a promise to suffer. Yes, to suffer; I will not take it back. You promised to suffer with. It made sense, because the person you married was likely to get hurt along the route, sooner or later, more or less, but hurt. And you promised to hurt with your spouse. A marriage is a life of shared pain.[5]

This shared suffering is a privilege! This is our ministry to one another! This is a reflection of the gift of marriage! How will you respond to this aspect of marriage?

If you are studying this book with your spouse, the best results can be obtained if you complete the following material individually and then discuss your answers together. As you compare ideas, feelings and attitudes, you will achieve new levels of communication and understanding in your marriage.

## What's Your Plan?

1. If you were going to describe your marriage with one word, what word would you use?

2. What word do you think your spouse would use to describe your marriage?

3. What benefits are you getting from your marriage relationship that you wouldn't have received if you had remained single? Be very specific.

4. What strengths do you see in your spouse? Have you ever told him or her that you are aware of these strengths and appreciate them?

5. What does your spouse do that makes you feel loved or valued?

6. What do you do that expresses your love and appreciation toward your spouse?

7. What are the strengths in your marriage? Who contributes most of these strengths?

8. What do you feel is the weakest area in your marriage? In what ways might you be responsible for this weak area?

9. What are you doing now to make your marriage a happy one?

*Notes*

1. David Small, *Marriage as Equal Partnership* (Grand Rapids, Mich.: Baker Book House, n.d.), pp. 41-43, 48, 49.

2. Judson Swihart, *How Do You Say, "I Love You"?* (Downers Grove, Ill.: Inter-Varsity Christian Fellowship of the U.S.A., 1977), n.p.

3. Source unknown.

4. David L. Luecke, *The Relationship Manual* (Columbia, Md.: The Relationship Institute, 1981), p. 25, adapted.

5. Lewis B. Smedes, *How Can It Be All Right When Everything Is All Wrong?* (San Francisco: Harper & Row, 1982), p. 61.

# WHAT MAKES A MARRIAGE WORK?

### CHAPTER THREE

Let's suppose you turned on your TV at the news hour and suddenly I came on the screen as the weather person. Of course you'd be surprised to see me there in the first place, but probably even more surprised when you heard what I had to say:

Tonight in place of the normal weather report and forecast, I would like to make a forecast for some of my viewers' marriages. For some of you, the forecast is cloudy skies with a 90-percent chance of thunder and lightning storms developing into tornadoes and hurricanes. There is no telling when they will end. In fact, there will be little relief in sight.

For other viewers, your marriages will have the normal adjustments and will go through the customary phases, but the weather outlook is brighter and clearer. When storm fronts do appear on the horizon, they won't last long and you will be prepared for them. You will (excuse the pun) weather them well.

And to add to the weather picture, I can tell you, the viewer, which of you will fit into the stormy forecast and which of you will fit into the good-weather forecast. But that's all the time we have right now. Tune in tomorrow for more details.

If I signed off like that, your TV set would probably get a boot thrown through it, the TV station would receive an irate phone call, and I would probably receive an invitation to be the next weather person at the North Pole. So to avoid all of the above, let me tell you which marriages have the best chance of fitting into the good-weather forecast. These are not just my own ideas; they have been gleaned from considerable research over the past few years.

I'm not just talking about marriages that stay together. Many of those marriages are empty shells. I'm talking about marriages that are fulfilling to both partners. Although I can't give a guarantee—a surefire formula—I can describe the characteristics of a healthy marriage.

## Portrait of a Healthy Marriage

### The Ability to Change and Tolerate Adjustments

Healthy marriages demonstrate flexibility on the part of both partners. Too many changes, however, bring disruption, along with a feeling of being out of control. This opens the door for anxiety. But like the captain of a sailing vessel thrown off course by a sudden wave, strong marriages involve people who are able to adjust and make course corrections that move back to a solid compass setting and return to the original course. Flexibility also means making personal changes for the benefit of the marriage. The big question is: How flexible are you? How flexible is your partner? If I were to ask you to give me some examples of your flexibility, what would you say?

### The Ability to Live with the Unalterable

Partners in a healthy marriage understand the necessity of living without all the answers to life and without having some problems totally resolved. This isn't always easy, especially for men, because they have a burning desire to feel in control of their lives.

Some personality characteristics and habits will never change. Perhaps your spouse will never remember to put the car seat back to the position you need when you drive, or to put the toilet seat down. Perhaps you will always put your clothes out the night before, which makes the room look cluttered. Perhaps your spouse will always gargle with the door open and miss the sink bowl most of the time. Are these major annoyances? Only if we view them that way. To have a good marriage we must be able to live with the imperfect. We have God as our role model; He loves us in spite of our imperfections.

### Belief in the Permanence of Marriage

In premarital counseling sessions I encourage couples to hold to the belief that their marriage will never end in divorce. It is simply not one of the options. "Till death do us part" is not a heavy, binding chain but a gratifying commitment. This means that during times of conflict, distance and anger, divorce is not even a consideration. As one person jokingly put it, "Divorce, no. Murder, maybe." When you hold to the belief that your marriage will last, it affects your approach to an imperfect spouse, to your

When you

hold to the

belief that

your marriage

will last, it

affects your

approach to

an imperfect

spouse, to

your

differences

and conflicts

and to

your future

together.

differences and conflicts and to your future together. Yes, it's true that the commitment level may not be the same for each partner. Commitment may ebb and flow from time to time, but it is there just the same.

## Trust in Each Other

When couples can depend and rely upon one another, they have a rare commodity desperately sought after in today's world. As one wife said, "I can depend upon my husband to keep his word. There's no flaking off or setting me up for failure. If he says he will be home at a certain time, he's either there or he calls me. I like that. It gives me a sense of security, and I feel freer with him because of that. Our intimacy level is strong because we trust one another."

## A Balance of Power

One of the main causes and perpetuators of conflict is the power struggle so common in marriages today. Marriage is based upon the recognition of the strengths and giftedness of each partner and the freedom to express such qualities in the marriage. It is a marriage of more or less equal power. Dependency and dominance (both used in a positive way here) shift back and forth between each partner.

## Enjoyment of Each Other

This means that both partners enjoy the other's presence—their silence and their talk, their values, faith and so on. Marriage is most satisfying when the spouses view each other as best friend. Such a friendship, like all friendships, takes time to cultivate and develop and also implies loyalty between the friends.

## Promotion of Personal Growth

Your marriage contains the power for personal growth in a way you've never dreamed of experiencing. I'm sure you would like that growth to be painless—like extracting a tooth with the aid of massive doses of Novocain. But no one yet has developed a marital Novocain. It doesn't exist. So get set, because some of the changes and growth will be painful.

Many couples struggle because marriage involves incredible work and effort. As one man said, "It's much more effort than I ever bargained for. I wanted a peaceful marriage. Harmony? I'm wondering if all the work and effort are worth the few times of peace and harmony we've ever experienced."

Let me ask you a question. How do you describe the conflicts in your life? In your marriage? Do you ever run out of words to describe what goes on? Do you have a vocabulary that would do justice to what you experience? I discovered the following synomyms for "conflict." You can find them yourself in any thesaurus. Underline any of the words that describe (or those that

The real issue is not whether you married the right person; it's more an issue of your being the right person for your spouse.

best describe) what it has been like in your marriage. The verbs include clash, disagree, discord, be at odds, spar, oppose, contend, lock horns, squabble, feud, bicker, wronged, struggle, tussle. Nouns include struggle, strife, warfare, Armageddon, fight, dispute, row, spat, quarrel. (In the final chapter we'll come back to resolving conflicts.)

## Facing Reality in Marriage

Many couples are surprised by marriage because they entered that relationship woefully unprepared. Their sense of reality was distorted by fantasy and wishful thinking. Some are surprised because they married in spite of unresolved past issues, hoping their partner would be their savior. Did you marry the person you thought you married?

I heard the story of a man who, after an intense and disappointing disagreement with his wife, felt quite frustrated and angry with her. After some time he came in and declared, "Janice, you're not the woman I married!" She turned and looked at him, and with a faint smile said, "I never was the woman you thought you married."

We tend to marry an illusion, a fantasy, an idealization projected onto a frail human being. Perhaps we marry a phantom or a dream, but when we reach out to touch that phantom, there's no substance. The real issue is not whether you married the right person; it's more an issue of your being the right person for your spouse. Zig Ziglar said it well:

> If you treat the wrong person like the right person, you could well end up having married the right person after all. On the other hand, if you marry the right person and treat that person wrong, you certainly will have ended up marrying the wrong person. I also know that it is far more important to be the right kind of person than it is to marry the right person. In short, whether you married the right or wrong person is primarily up to you.[1]

One of the initial adjustments in marriage is facing the realities of marriage. The good news is that your conflicts subside when this happens. Besides, facing reality isn't all that bad.

> People can let go of fantasy if they realize that "reality" is not a code word for "trouble." Among other things, reality means accepting the fun of planning a future with another person you respect and love. It is the joy of living with your best friend and the security of catching a whopping cold and having a spouse on hand to make chicken soup without complaining. Reality is having a disagreement and coming to grips with the notion that you and your spouse may never see eye-to-eye on a number of issues.[2]

If there is ever a place in which we need the grace of God to face life's realities, it is marriage. None of us has the capability of making it by ourselves. Consider this: Your marriage will make it not because of what you and your spouse do; it will make it because of the grace of God! We may have married because of our love for the other person, but none of us knew what that love was all about. Perhaps we hoped our courtship love would sustain and carry us throughout the years of marriage. We were hoping to relax and enjoy our love. Mike Mason has written one of the most thought-provoking books on this subject, *The Mystery of Marriage*. He says:

> To be married is not to be taken off the front lines of love, but rather, to be plunged into the thick of things. It is to be faced, day in and day out, with the necessity of making over and over again, and at deeper and deeper levels, that same terrifyingly momentous and impossible decision which one could only have made when one was head over heels in love and out of one's mind with trust and faith. This is not resignation to a fate, but the free and spontaneous embracing of a gift, of a challenge and a destiny.
>
> Is it any wonder if people cannot take the pressure? It is a pressure that can only be handled by love, and in ever-increasing doses. Marriage involves a continuous daily renewal of a decision which, since it is of such a staggering order as to be humanly impossible to make, can only be made through the grace of God.[3]

At first, couples blissfully assume their partners want nothing more than to act and think and feel exactly as they do. When they discover this is not the case, it seems as though something terrible has occurred. But not really. Mourning this loss carries with it the acceptance of differences in character, personality, communication style, values and sexual desire. Eventually, acceptance and adjustment lessen conflict. I would rather see some conflict occur so resolution happens instead of couples' burying issues until they again rise out of control, infused with new power and pain.

The storms in your marriage have various starting points. They may be present because of your past experience with your parents or because you entered marriage believing in too many myths. The storms may be there because of not knowing how to grow and develop new ways of responding at the present time. No matter what the reasons, you can overcome the hindrances.

What myths did you believe about marriage? Some of the more common myths are:

I thought my spouse would be an extension of my own emotional and physical needs. And when my needs weren't met right away and in the way I wanted, I felt ripped off! I got angry! How dare that person not meet my needs!

I expected my marriage to be problem free. After all, good Christian marriages just don't have problems or conflict. Nobody told me that good marriages become good marriages through constructive conflict.

I expected my spouse to know what I wanted or needed. Why spend a lot of time talking about what you want? Once you're married, your spouse ought to know.

# What Do You Think?

1. Write or draw a weather report describing your marriage.
2. What myths or misbeliefs did you carry into marriage?
3. What happened to the myths? Did they die? Did they receive a proper burial, or do they go through a periodic resurrection?

Perhaps you're like one couple who came to see me. They didn't want to take at face value what I told them, for they asked, "Norm, undoubtedly what you just shared with us is based on research. What was it that was described as positive, and what was negative? I think it would help us to know the specifics."

# How to Encourage Positive Interaction

They were right. Stable couples suggest numerous ways to express positive interaction in marriage. And time and time again, the Word of God admonishes us to behave in a positive and encouraging way.

And become useful and helpful and kind to one another, tenderhearted (compassionate, understanding, loving-hearted), forgiving one another [readily and freely], as God in Christ forgave you (Eph. 4:32, *AMP*).

So, chosen by God for this new life of love, dress in the wardrobe God picked out for you: compassion, kindness, humility, quiet strength, discipline. Be even-tempered, content with second place, quick to forgive an offense.

Forgive as quickly and completely as the Master forgave you. And regardless of what else you put on, wear love. It's your basic, all-purpose garment. Never be without it (Col. 3:12,13, *THE MESSAGE*).

## A Listening Attitude

It's important to show interest in your partner as a person, to discover what he or she has experienced during the day and to uncover any upset feelings. This can involve listening and looking at each other—without glancing at the TV or the paper on your lap. It can mean listening—without attempting to fix a problem your spouse is sharing with you, unless you are asked to do so. If you're a man, it can mean giving more verbal responses and feedback when you listen, because women like to hear this so they know that you're listening. James 1:19 (*AMP*) says to be "a ready listener."

## Frequent Affection in a Variety of Ways

Being consistently affectionate—not just at those times when one is interested in sex—is a highly valued positive response. Sometimes nothing is shared verbally. It can just mean sitting side by side and touching gently, or moving close enough that you barely touch while you watch the sun dip over a mountain and color the clouds a reddish glow. It could mean reaching out and holding hands in public. It can mean doing something thoughtful, unrequested and noticed only by your partner. (But since I've mentioned the subject of sex, I would *highly encourage* every man to read and apply the content of Joyce and Cliff Penner's insightful book *Men and Sex*. It could transform your physical relationship.)

When your spouse has had a rough day, you may choose just to stroke her head or rub his shoulders instead of talking about the details of the day. Being understood by your partner to this degree and having your needs met give you the assurance that you have indeed married the right person.

Affection is demonstrated in many ways. Years ago I heard the story of a couple who had been invited to a potluck dinner. The wife was not known for her cooking ability, but she decided to cook a custard pie. As they drove to the dinner, they knew they were in trouble, for they smelled the scorched crust. Then, when they turned a corner, the contents of the pie shifted dramatically from one side of the pie shell to the other. He could see her anxiety rising by the moment.

When they arrived, they placed the pie on the dessert table. The guests served themselves salad and then went back for the main course. Just before they could move on to the desserts, the husband marched up to the table, looked over the number of homemade desserts and snatched up his wife's pie. As others looked at him, he announced, "There are so many desserts here, and my wife so rarely makes my favorite dessert; I'm claiming this for myself. I ate light on all the other courses so now I can be a glutton."

And a glutton he was. Later his wife said, "He sat by the door eating what he could, mushing up the rest so no one else would bug him for a piece, and slipping chunks to the hosts' Rottweiler when no one was looking. He saw me looking at him and gave me a big wink. What he did made my evening. My husband, who doesn't always say much, communicated more love with what he did than with any words he could ever say."

## Kindness and Care

Of course there are many other ways to show you care. I raise flowers all year long, and I know Joyce enjoys seeing them inside the house. Often, after I've made the coffee, I cut her a rose and put it in a vase by her coffee cup. It has almost become automatic now, but the motivation is the same. And often before I travel, Joyce slips a love note into my pants pocket.

Perhaps you're in the store and you see a favorite food your spouse enjoys, and you buy it for him or her, even if you hate it. Or you decide to stop at the store for an item, and you call your spouse at home or work to see if there's anything he or she wants or needs. You are thinking of others rather than thinking of yourself. You are following through with the scriptural teaching in Ephesians 4:32 (*NIV*): "Be kind and compassionate to one another."

An act of caring can be a phone call to ask if your partner has a prayer request. Acts of caring can mean remembering special dates and anniversaries without being reminded. I'm amazed at the number of wives who have been deeply hurt by their husbands who didn't remember anniversaries or even birthdays.

And the husbands' excuses are so lame. "I just didn't remember," "I need to be reminded," or "We just didn't do that in our family." If the husband is sitting in my counseling office, I simply ask him if he forgets to go to work or get involved in his hobby. Reluctantly, he says no, and I go on to let him know that I believe he's capable of learning something new that will benefit both him and his wife. We don't accept excuses when change is the obvious step.

## Appreciative Words

Another positive response is to show appreciation. This means going out of your way to notice all the little things your partner does and letting him or her know you appreciate it. It also means focusing on the positive experiences and dwelling upon those rather than the negative (more will be said about this later). Working toward agreement and appreciating the other's perspective is important. Compliments convey appreciation, but they need to be balanced between what a person does and who he or she is. Affirmations based on the qualities of a person are rare but highly appreciated.

Showing genuine concern for your spouse when you notice he or she is upset builds unity and intimacy in a relationship. You may not be able to do anything, but sharing your desire to do so may be all that is necessary. Being apologetic rather than defensive is another expression of affection. When your partner shares a problem with you, don't relate a similar problem you once had, tell him what to do, crack jokes to cheer him up or ask how he got into that problem in the first place. Instead, listen, put your arm around him, show that you understand, and let him know it's all right to feel and act the way he does.

Show empathy. This is the feeling of being with another person both emotionally and intellectually. It is viewing life through your spouse's eyes, feeling as he or she feels and hearing your mate's story through his or her perceptions.

In marriage you have a choice to respond with empathy, sympathy or apathy. Sympathy is being overinvolved in the emotions of your spouse. It can actually undermine your emotional strength. Apathy means you couldn't care less. But empathy includes rapport—knowing how your spouse would feel in most situations, without having to ask. You experience something together, at the same time, through the eyes of your partner.

## Free to Be

Acceptance of our spouses means letting them know that even though we might not agree with what they're saying, we're willing to hear them out. It means we free our partners from being molded into the fantasy we want them to be. This is more than tolerance. It is sending the message: "You and I are different in many ways. It's all right for you to be you and for me to be me. As we learn to complement each other, we're stronger together than we are separately." It is inevitable that we will help to change each other. But the purpose for which this is done, and the method, makes a world of difference.

## Frequent Laughter

A sense of humor and being able to laugh, joke and have fun give balance to the serious side of marriage. Some of what you laugh at will be private, and some things will be shared with others. Having a sense of humor means you're able to laugh at yourself (even if it takes awhile sometimes!), and the two of you can laugh together. Sometimes the best memories are those hilarious incidents that happen even though your partner didn't think it was funny at the time.

Several years ago, while speaking at a family camp at Forest Home, California, such an event happened to Joyce and me. We were staying in a nice cabin. Since I'm an early riser, I went down to the dining hall for an early breakfast. Joyce got up a little later and didn't eat a large breakfast, knowing that I would bring her back some fruit and a muffin. I entered the cabin and was just about ready to go into the bedroom with her food when the door of the bathroom swung open. Joyce, fresh out of the shower, said, "Don't go in there! It's still there! Don't take my food in there!"

I was shocked and said, "What? What's in there?"

"In there!" she said again, almost in tears now. "It's still in the bedroom. It was terrible. And don't you dare laugh. It wasn't funny!" I still didn't know what she was talking about.

Finally, she calmed down and told me what happened. She had been resting in bed, drinking her coffee, when she reached down to pick up her slippers. She found one, lifted it up, and thrust her hand under the bed to find the other one. Now, Forest Home was using new humane mousetraps that consisted of a 6x6-inch piece of cardboard with an extremely sticky substance on it. When a mouse stuck in it, it was stuck permanently and would eventually die. You can guess what happened. Not only did Joyce put her hand directly on the goo substance, but on a bloated, dead mouse! It was gross! (I have a picture of it.) As she said, she went ballistic with screams, trying to dislodge this disgusting creature from her hand.

As Joyce was telling me this, she was shaking her hand and demonstrating how she had tried to dislodge the mouse. The more she shook her hand, the funnier it got. I was biting the inside of my mouth to keep from smiling—all the time remembering those fateful words, "Don't you dare laugh. It wasn't funny." I think she saw my struggle because, with an exaggerated pout, she looked at me and said slowly, "*It's not funny.*"

That's all it took. I was a dead man and I knew it. I laughed until the tears rolled down my face. I did take the mouse out and got rid of it. I also told Joyce that I would have gone into hysterics as well, if that had happened to me, and that she had every right to be upset. After several hugs she said, "I guess it was pretty funny at that." Now it's one of our favorite stories.

We also have many funny memories in which I was the source of amusement. Just ask Joyce sometime.

## Joy in Common

A related positive in marriage is the sense of shared joy.[4] You share your partner's excitement and delight and you want your partner to be aware of what you're experiencing as well. Joy is a sense of gladness, not necessarily happiness. It's also a command from Scripture. We are to "rejoice with those who rejoice" (Rom. 12:15, *NIV*).

## A Grateful Heart

Another positive is never becoming complacent or taking one another for granted. A friend of mine described it this way:

> People in long-term marriages tend to take each other for granted. The most common of the "takens" include:
>
> You will always be here for me.
> You will always love me.
> You will always be able to provide for me.
> You will always be the same.
> We will always be together.
>
> Making these assumptions in a marriage is living more in fantasyland than on reality ridge. People who take things for granted are seldom appreciative of the every-day blessings in their lives. After a time, they come to believe life owes them these little gifts. They seldom say thank you for anything.
>
> When you take someone for granted, you demean him or her. You send the unspoken message, *You are not worth much to me.* You also rob this person of the gift of human appreciation. And to be loved and appreciated gives all of us a reason to live each day. When that gift is withdrawn or denied over the years, our spirits with-er and die. People may endure this hardship and stay

married forever, but they are only serving a sentence. In long-term marriages where one or both spouses are continually taken for granted, a wall of indifference arises between husband and wife. The longer the marriage, the higher the wall and the greater the human isolation. The way out of this woodpile is simple but crucial:

- Start saying thank you and showing appreciation for anything and everything.
- Be more consciously tuned in to what is going on around you.
- Become more giving and affirming.
- Specialize in the many little things that mean a lot: Bring each other flowers, take long walks in the country, lie on the floor in front of the fireplace, prepare breakfast in bed for each other, hold hands in public, walk in the rain, send caring and funny cards to each other in the mail, buy each other small gifts for no apparent reason.

Remember: A thirty-five-year marriage does not guarantee year number thirty-six. Take nothing for granted just because you have it today.[5]

Keep in mind, in a healthy marriage . . .

> You look out for "number 2" rather than number 1
> You energize your spouse rather than drain energy from him or her
> You eliminate blaming and shaming from the marriage
> You are willing to learn from your partner
> You end your disagreements with a feeling of resolve
> You feel better after a disagreement[6]

### Bilingual Communication

There is one final factor. Those couples who learn to flex and speak their spouse's language will have the best communication of all. It may sound a bit strange, but over the last 32 years of counseling couples and conducting marriage-enrichment seminars I'm even more convinced that this is the heart of the communication process. It means you accept your differences, discover the uniqueness of your partner's communication vocabulary, patterns and style, and begin to use them as you share together. It works in marriage and it works in the business world as well.

No, you don't give up being who you are or your usual way of communicating. It's a matter of adding to your repertoire of responses so that you have a greater range. Most individuals like to talk with others who speak the same language. You can learn to do this. I did. And what a difference it makes! That's what the rest of this book is about.

## What's Your Plan?

These are just some of the positives that keep a marriage alive. But what about you? On a scale of 0 to 10, how would you rate the presence of these positives in your own marriage (0 being nonexistent and 10 being superabundant)? How would your spouse rate these positives? (In the appendix you will find a marriage assessment form that will enable you to take a fresh look at your marriage.)

*Notes*
1. Zig Ziglar, *Sermons Illustrated*, April 1993.
2. Maxine Rock, *The Marriage Rock* (Atlanta: Peachtree Publishers, 1986), pp. 78, 79.

3. Mike Mason, *The Mystery of Marriage* (Portland, Oreg.: Multnomah Press, 1985), pp. 55, 56.

4. John Gottman with Nan Silver, *Why Marriages Succeed or Fail* (New York: Simon & Schuster, 1994), pp. 58-61, adapted.

5. Jim Smoke, *Facing 50* (Nashville, Tenn.: Thomas Nelson Publishers, 1994), pp. 40, 41.

6. Paul Pearsall, *The Ten Laws of Lasting Love* (New York: Simon & Schuster, 1993), pp. 298, 299.

# THE KEY TO
# INTIMACY

CHAPTER FOUR

Communication is the link that creates a relationship between people. Communication helps us become who and what we are and what we know. The process of communicating can be clear, which leads to understanding—or unclear, which leads to confusion.

Every person who marries brings his or her own dictionary to the marriage. Unless definitions are clarified, the words we speak to each other cannot be understood. A message shared between you and your spouse can be easily misinterpreted, depending on how it is worded (words omitted or too many words) or simply because it is incorrectly received by your partner. Sometimes even a written message gets messed up, such as the following ad that appeared in the classified ads section of a small-town newspaper on a Monday:

FOR SALE: R. D. Jones has one sewing machine for sale. Phone 958 after 7 P.M. and ask for Mrs. Kelly who lives with him cheap.

On Tuesday—NOTICE: We regret having erred in R. D. Jones's ad yesterday. It should have read: One sewing machine for sale. Cheap. Phone 958 and ask for Mrs. Kelly who lives with him after 7 P.M.

On Wednesday—R. D. Kelly has informed us that he has received several annoying telephone calls because of the error we made in his classified ad yesterday. His ad stands corrected as follows: FOR SALE: R. D. Jones has one sewing machine for sale. Cheap. Phone 958 after 7 P.M. and ask for Mrs. Kelly who lives with him.

Finally on Thursday—NOTICE: I, R. D. Jones, have no sewing machine for sale. I smashed it. Don't call 958 as the telephone has been taken out. I have not been carrying on with Mrs. Kelly. Until yesterday she was my housekeeper, but she quit.[1]

Before giving a definition, remember that when you and your spouse are communicating, there is more than just one message. There are actually six, and this is where the problem arises.

First, you have something you *want to get across* to the other person—what you mean. Perhaps you've thought about it, or you just formulate it as you open your mouth. But it may not come out the way you intended. So the second message is what you *actually say*. Now, let's turn to your spouse. The third message is what the your spouse *actually hears* while filtering and processing the information, which leads to the fourth message—what your spouse *thinks he or she hears!* Uh-oh, now the possibility of misunderstanding increases.

If the communication stopped here, it wouldn't be so complicated. But the fifth message is what your spouse *says about what you said*. Now it's back in your lap, because the sixth message is what you *think your spouse said about what you said.*

Discouraging? Rather. But it does illustrate why so often communication is hard work. We want the other person not only to listen but to understand what we mean. The old proverb, "Say what you mean and mean what you say," is a worthy goal, but not an easy one to achieve.

It would be so much easier if each of you spoke one another's language (more about that later in the book).

## What Do You Think?

Here are four questions to help you think about yourself as a communicator.

1. What is your personal definition of the word "communication"?_____

2. Is communicating with your spouse difficult for you?
   Often          Sometimes          Almost          Never

3. Does your mate seem to have difficulty understanding what you mean?
   Often          Sometimes          Almost          Never

4. What do you think your mate would say about your ability to communicate?
   Great          So-So          Well . . .

Consider this definition of communication: It is the process of sharing yourself verbally and nonverbally with another person in such a way that both of you understand and accept what you say.

The second part of the definition involves listening on the part of the receiver (an entire chapter will be devoted to this important topic). Acceptance doesn't mean agreement; but the listener can accept that what you say is the way you see things—the way you believe or feel about something.

Everyone communicates. It's impossible to *not* communicate. Some people say the longer they are married the less they need to talk about certain issues because they know each other so well. Could it be that the longer a couple is married, the more they learn what *not* to talk about? Is there any subject in your marriage relationship that needs to be talked about that isn't being talked about?

There are numerous books, programs, seminars and articles available on communication—guidelines on what to say, how to say it, how not to say it, 17 better ways to say it and so on. All the help you've ever wanted or haven't wanted is available. But what if we didn't have any of these helps—not even one? What if we only had one resource to give us communication guidelines? And what if that one resource was the Bible—the Word of God? Would it be sufficient? Let's look at just the biblical teaching on communication.

## The Power of Words

### What We Say to Others

Scripture is clear that our words have tremendous power. Our words can heal, support and comfort, or they can wound.

> A bit in the mouth of a horse controls the whole horse.
> A small rudder on a huge ship in the hands of a skilled
> captain sets a course in the face of the strongest winds.

A word out of your mouth may seem of no account, but it can accomplish nearly anything—or destroy it!

It only takes a spark, remember, to set off a forest fire. A careless or wrongly placed word out of your mouth can do that. By our speech we can ruin the world, turn harmony to chaos, throw mud on a reputation, send the whole world up in smoke and go up in smoke with it, smoke right from the pit of hell.

This is scary: You can tame a tiger, but you can't tame a tongue—it's never been done. The tongue runs wild, a wanton killer. With our tongues we bless God our Father; with the same tongues we curse the very men and women he made in his image. Curses and blessings out of the same mouth! (Jas. 3:3-10, *THE MESSAGE*).

As far as power is concerned, James compares the power of the tongue to the rudder of a ship. Comparatively speaking, a rudder is a small part of the ship, yet it can turn the ship in any direction and control its destiny. What a husband and wife say to one another can turn their marriage in different directions (and in some cases cause them to wind up going in a vicious circle).

Continuing to emphasize the tongue's potency, James compares it to a flame of fire. Great forests can be leveled by one tiny spark. In the same way, a marriage can be damaged and/or even set on fire by one remark or, more typically, by continually chopping and snipping away at each other.

Words do spread like fire. Did you ever try to stop a rumor? Did you ever attempt to squelch an unkind story once it was told? Impossible! Who can unsay words or wipe out what has been heard?

James continues to bear down when he writes that man's ingenuity has succeeded in taming almost every kind of living

Controlling the tongue needs to be a continuing aim for every husband and wife because *everything* that is said either helps or hinders, heals or scars, builds up or tears down.

creature, yet he has failed in taming his own tongue! To tame means to control and to render useful and beneficial. Man has not been able to do that with his tongue on any widespread basis.

Each person must be responsible for his own tongue-training program. Controlling the tongue needs to be a continuing aim for every husband and wife because *everything* that is said either helps or hinders, heals or scars, builds up or tears down.

According to Scripture, the husband or wife who blurts out whatever he or she is thinking or feeling without considering the consequences is in a bad way indeed: "Do you see a man who is hasty in his words? There is more hope for a fool than for him" (Prov. 29:20).

First Peter 3:10 (*TLB*) sums it up nicely: "If you want a happy, good life, keep control of your tongue, and guard your lips." Control of your tongue is not easy to accomplish in your own strength, but if you depend on the Holy Spirit for teaching and guidance, you will have help and strength far beyond your own.

Remember how good it feels when you have a building-up kind of conversation with your spouse? You concentrate on choosing words that are kind and appropriate for the time and purpose. And your spouse does the same. The result is that you encourage each other and create a rewarding situation for yourselves. Proverbs 25:11 (*RSV*) describes the beauty of such a moment: "A word fitly spoken is like apples of gold in a setting of silver." If we put this last verse in everyday language, we would say, "The right word at the right time, how good it is!"

In the book of Job we find a situation that perhaps most of us have experienced. Job had three friends who endlessly talked *at* him. Finally, in frustration, he cried out, "How long will you vex and torment me and break me in pieces with your words?" (Job 19:2, *AMP*).

Perhaps all these verses are here to warn us: Be careful with your words. Guard your mouth! *Your words come from your mind.*

### What We Say to Ourselves

Every day we carry on conversations with ourselves. It's all right. It doesn't mean we're odd or on the verge of spacing out. It's normal to talk to oneself.

But are you aware that:

Most of your emotions—such as anger, depression, guilt, worry—are initiated and escalated by your self-talk?

The way you behave toward your spouse is determined by your self-talk and not by his or her behavior (or thought life)?

What you say, and how you say it, is a direct expression of what you say to yourself?

Self-talk is what you tell yourself—the words you say to your-self about yourself, your spouse, your experiences, the past, the future, God.

Self-talk, or your inner conversation, is not an emotion or feeling, and it is not an attitude. However, repetitive self-talk *turns into* attitudes, values and beliefs.

Many of your thoughts are automatic. You don't sit around thinking about what you're going to do next. Thoughts slide into your consciousness so smoothly that you don't sense their entrance. Many of them are stimulated from past experience, attitudes and beliefs. You build up storehouses of memories and experience, retaining and remembering those things you con-centrate on most.

The Scriptures have much to say about thinking and our thought life. The words "think," "thought" and "mind" are used over 300 times in the Bible. Proverbs 23:7 says, "As he thinks within himself, so he is."

Often the Scriptures refer to our heart as the source of our thoughts:

> The mind of the [uncompromisingly] righteous studies how to answer, but the mouth of the wicked pours out evil things (Prov. 15:28, *AMP*).

> But the things that come out of the mouth come from the heart, and these make a man "unclean." For out of the heart come evil thoughts, murder, adultery, sexual immorality, theft, false testimony, slander (Matt. 15:18,19, *NIV*).

God knows the content of our thoughts: "All the ways of a man are pure in his own eyes, but the Lord weighs the spirits (the thoughts and intents of the heart)" (Prov 16:2, *AMP*). So, how are your thoughts? Do you see the connection between what's occurring inside you and what you say? It's something to become *very* aware of for the health of your marital relationship.

There is good news: Our thought life can come under the control of the Holy Spirit. First Peter 1:13 tells us to gird up our minds. This takes mental exertion, putting out of our minds anything that would hinder progress in our marriages. God's Word tells us what to concentrate on: "Finally, brethren, whatever is true, whatever is honorable, whatever is right, whatever is pure, whatever is lovely, whatever is of good repute, if there is any excellence and if anything worthy of praise, let your mind dwell on these things" (Phil. 4:8).

## What Do You Think?

1. List some of your thoughts that affect communication with your spouse.
2. Which of the Scripture passages already mentioned would help your communication process if you followed their teachings?

### Think Before You Speak

Do you remember the old statement, "Make sure your brain is in gear before you engage your mouth"? That's basically what God's Word is saying.

So often we think, *Uh-oh, I wish I hadn't said that. I'd like to take it back.* But once the words are spoken, it's done. There's no erase button, no rewind button. There's no judge telling the jury to disregard that last comment.

When you take the time to think before you speak, you can evaluate, edit and consider the impact of your words on the other person.

What would happen in a marriage if the following principles were consistently applied?

Careless words stab like a sword, but wise words bring healing (Prov. 12:18, *NCV*).

Patient people have great understanding, but people with quick tempers show their foolishness (Prov. 14:29, *NCV*).

Those who are careful about what they say keep themselves out of trouble (Prov. 21:23, *NCV*).

Do you see people who speak too quickly? There is more hope for a foolish person than for them (Prov. 29:20, *NCV*).

## Speak the Truth

We live in a culture that believes it's all right to lie. Today we call it "modifying" the truth.

What do we mean by this? To modify means to change. Thus, what is changed is no longer true but a lie. Isn't it all right to lie if it means you can avoid unpleasantness in your relationship with a person? We can all think of situations in which we feel it would be best not to speak the truth for fear of hurting the other person. But does lying really avoid unpleasantness? A lie is usually discovered and then there is even more unpleasantness. Besides, who are we really afraid of hurting—the other person or ourselves? We have to be honest with ourselves about our motivation. Often, we find it easy to lie if we can ease out of an unpleasant situation.

Perhaps the most tempting opportunity to lie is when we're confronted with something we've done. We feel like altering the truth or rationalizing it in order to push the blame away from ourselves. You can see this pattern starting in small children. When they are confronted with a wrong action, they find it so difficult to say, "Yes, I did it. I'm sorry. I accept the responsibility." Have you ever noticed the other person's reaction when you accept responsibility for your actions and are open and truthful? The person is amazed, even shocked!

Is it possible to tell the truth and yet hold back part of it because the other person is not ready for all the facts? Perhaps. But does holding back part of the information cause the person to think the opposite of what the truth actually is? That's something to think about!

What happens when your wife walks in and asks, "How do you like my new dress? How does it look on me?" Often a husband will

There is a close correlation between truth and trust in a relationship. Truth must be accompanied by love, tact and deep concern for the other person.

say, "Fine," even though he doesn't like the dress and it doesn't look good on his wife. Let's hope the wife was being truthful in asking the question! Was she looking for an answer to her question or was she wanting her ego built up? We also can be deceitful by the questions we ask! In this situation it would be better if the husband honestly shared his feelings. Marriage is built on trust, and there can be no trust unless there is truthfulness. Answering a question like this, as well as hundreds of others in marriage, requires tact! "I think I've seen you in other dresses I like better" is a much better response than "Huh! It sure shows off your weight!"

Scripture gives us a pattern to follow regarding modification of the truth. Read and discuss Proverbs 6:16-19; 12:17; 28:23; Ephesians 4:15,25; and Colossians 3:9.

Notice Ephesians 4:15, which exhorts us to speak the truth in love. The words "in love" could imply tact! Be concerned about how you speak the truth. Be sensitive to the other person and the ways in which you can make him receptive to words of truth. Do not rip the person apart and scar him emotionally by frank, honest words that carry a tinge of brutality! Truth must be accompanied by love, tact and deep concern for the other person. There is a close correlation between truth and trust in a relationship.

## What Do You Think?

1. When is the most difficult time for you to share all that you believe or feel?
2. What could your spouse do to help you share more openly?

## Avoid Quarreling

> What is causing the quarrels and fights among you?
> Isn't it because there is a whole army of evil desires with-
> in you? You want what you don't have, so you kill to get
> it. You long for what others have, and can't afford it, so
> you start a fight to take it away from them. And yet the
> reason you don't have what you want is that you don't
> ask God for it. And even when you do ask you don't get
> it because your whole aim is wrong—you want only what
> will give *you* pleasure (James 4:1-3, *TLB*).

Does this Scripture mean that couples aren't going to have
conflicts? Not at all. Two unique and different individuals cannot come together without adjustment and conflict. The individual tastes, preferences, habits, likes and dislikes, personality
differences, values and standards will confront each other. But
remember, conflict is not the same as quarreling. Disagreeing is
not the same as quarreling.

Verbal conflict in itself is not harmful; it can open doors of
communication. On the other hand, a quarrel is defined as verbal strife in which the emotions have taken over and the focus is
more on the other person than on resolving the problem. When
the quarrel is over, there is usually a greater distance between the
couple or a residual bad feeling. (Conflict resolution will be cov-
ered in the last chapter.)

The Word of God is specific about what to do with quarrels:

> People without good sense find fault with their neigh-
> bors, but those with understanding keep quiet (Prov.
> 11:12, *NCV*).

Starting a quarrel is like a leak in a dam, so stop it before a fight breaks out (Prov. 17:14, *NCV*).

Foolish people are always fighting, but avoiding quarrels will bring you honor (Prov. 20:3, *NCV*).

Just as charcoal and wood keep a fire going, a quarrelsome person keeps an argument going (Prov. 26:21, *NCV*).

If it is possible, as far as it depends on you, live at peace with everyone (Rom. 12:18, *NIV*).

Get rid of all bitterness, rage and anger, brawling and slander, along with every form of malice (Eph. 4:31, *NIV*).

Make every effort to live in peace with all men and to be holy; without holiness no one will see the Lord (Heb. 12:14, *NIV*).

## Avoid Criticizing

Criticism is a special brand of communication that cuts and destroys. Its purpose is *not* to resolve conflict or draw a spouse closer. It's a way to feel justified and superior. It's a way to release anger. Every time you criticize, you find fault. You're saying to the other person, "You're defective in some way and I don't accept you." Criticism does have an effect on the other person; he or she will turn you off, counterattack or become resentful. Criticism is a no-brainer. It doesn't work. It's ineffective. God's Word is clear on the issue:

Then let us no more criticize and blame and pass judgment on one another, but rather decide and endeavor never to put a stumbling block or an obstacle or a hindrance in the way of a brother (Rom. 14:13, *AMP*).

Why do you look at the speck of sawdust in your brother's eye and pay no attention to the plank in your own eye? How can you say to your brother, "Let me take the speck out of your eye," when all the time there is a plank in your own eye? (Matt. 7:3,4, *NIV*).

All couples will have complaints to voice from time to time. That's normal. Complaints, however, can be voiced in a way that a spouse will hear them and not become defensive. For example, instead of focusing upon what annoys you, talk more about what you would *appreciate* your spouse doing. Your partner will be much more likely to hear you and consider your request. Talking about what you don't like just reinforces the possibility of its continuance with even greater intensity. The principle of pointing your partner toward what you would like conveys that you believe he or she is capable of doing what you have requested. If you do this consistently, along with giving praise and appreciation when your spouse complies, you will see a change. This way of relating to your spouse accomplishes much more than criticism. The same dynamic applies to children. The power of praise can never be underestimated.

I've also seen this principle work in the raising of our golden retriever, Sheffield—not that I'm comparing people to dogs. Sheffield was trained in the basics when he was four months old and now brings in the paper, takes items back and forth to Joyce and me, "answers" the phone and brings it to me, and picks up items off the floor and puts them in the trash. All it took was ignoring the times when he didn't do it right and giving praise and hugs when he came through. If I had criticized him I would have destroyed his spirit.

I don't think we are much different in this respect. Affirming and encouraging responses can literally change our lives because we want and need others to believe in us. An unusual example of this affirmation is found in the Babemba tribe in southern Africa. When one of the tribal members has acted irresponsibly, he or she is taken to the center of the village. Everyone in the village stops work and gathers in a large circle around the person. In turn, each person, regardless of age, speaks to the person and recounts the good things he or she has done. All the positive incidents in the person's life, plus the good attributes, strengths and kindnesses, are recalled with accuracy and detail. Not one word about the problem behaviors is even mentioned.

This ceremony, which sometimes lasts for several days, isn't complete until every positive expression has been spoken by those assembled. The person in the circle is literally flooded with affirmation, then welcomed back into the tribe. Can you imagine how the person feels about himself or herself? Can you imagine the person's desire to continue to reflect those positive qualities? Perhaps a variation of this ceremony is needed in marriages and families today.

Criticism is the initial negative response that opens the door for other destructive responses to follow. Criticism is different from complaint because it attacks a person's personality and character, usually with blame. Most criticism is overgeneralized ("You always . . .") and personally accusing (the word "you" is central and the word "should" is given prominence).

# Various Forms of Criticism

## Joking

Criticism can be hidden under the camouflage of humor. When confronted about it, a person will avoid the responsibility by saying, "Hey, I was just joking." It reminds me of the passage in Proverbs: "Like a madman shooting deadly, burning arrows is the one who tricks a neighbor and then says, 'I was just joking'" (Prov. 26:18,19, *NCV*).

## Faultfinding

Faultfinding is a favorite response of the perfectionistic spouse. Criticism is usually destructive, but it's interesting to hear those who criticize say they're just trying to remold their partner into a better person by offering some "constructive" criticism. All too often criticism doesn't construct, it demolishes. It doesn't nourish a relationship, it poisons. Often the presentation is like this description: "There is one who speaks rashly like the thrusts of a sword" (Prov. 12:18). Destructive criticism accuses, tries to make the other feel guilty, intimidates and is often an outgrowth of personal resentment.

## Zingers

Criticism comes in many shapes and sizes. You've heard of zingers—those lethal verbally guided missiles. A zinger comes at you with a sharp point and a jagged barb that catches the flesh as it goes in. The power of these caustic statements is apparent when you realize that one zinger can undo 20 acts of kindness. That's right, 20!

Once a zinger has landed, the effect is similar to a radioactive cloud that settles on an area of what used to be prime farmland. The land is so contaminated by the radioactivity that even though seeds are scattered and plants are planted, they fail to take root. They subsequently die out or are washed away by the elements. It takes decades for the contamination to dissipate.

Loving words following the placement of a zinger find a similar hostile soil. It may take hours before there is receptivity or positive response to your positive overtures.[2]

### Invalidating Words

Another form of criticism is called invalidation and is often the cause of marital distress. When invalidation is present in a marriage, it destroys the effect of *validation*, as well as the friendship relationship of marriage. Sometimes couples get along and maintain their relationship without sufficient validation, but they cannot handle continual invalidation. This is yet another example of one negative comment destroying 20 acts of kindness.[3]

Invalidation is like a slow, fatal disease that, once established in a relationship, spreads and destroys the positive feelings. As one wife said, "The so-called friend I married became my enemy with his unexpected attacks. I felt demeaned, put down, and my self-esteem slowly crumbled. I guess that's why our fights escalated so much. I had to fight to survive."

To keep love and your marriage alive, keep the criticism out of it.

## What's Your Plan?

1. When was the last time you quarreled with your spouse? How was the quarrel resolved?
2. What could you do differently the next time?
3. Describe how you feel when you are criticized.

4. Describe how you can turn criticism into positive comments.

*Notes*
1. Sven Wahlroos, *Family Communication* (New York: Harper & Row, 1974), p. 3.
2. Clifford Notarius and Howard Markman, *We Can Work It Out* (New York: G. P. Putnam's Sons, 1993), p. 28, adapted.
3. Ibid., pp. 123, 124, adapted.

# THE FINER POINTS OF COMMUNICATION

### CHAPTER FIVE

It's a wall that pushes others away. It makes a statement about your desire to grow. It blocks communication. What is it? *Defensiveness.*

"I didn't do that; you just think I did."

"You're the one who never listens . . . don't point a finger at me."

Defensiveness has many forms and flavors: No matter what your spouse says, you deny it or insist you're not the one to blame. Or you make excuses: "The dog ate the list you gave me." Or you manifest a defensive attitude in your body language.

You can view your spouse's words (complaints or concerns) either as an attack or as information that is strongly expressed. The choice is yours. But if you're following the Bible as your guide for communication, hear this: You need to admit when you're wrong.

# Admit Your Mistakes

A lot of people find it difficult if not impossible to say: "I'm wrong; you may be right." If necessary, practice saying this sentence so that you will be able to say it when it fits a disagreement or discussion with your spouse. When you honestly own up to knowing that you are wrong and the other person is right, you improve communication a thousandfold and deepen your relationship with your spouse.

When appropriate, ask for forgiveness. James tells us to admit our faults to one another and to pray for each other (see James 5:16).

Proverbs 28:13 (*TLB*) has good advice: "A man who refuses to admit his mistakes can never be successful. But if he confesses and forsakes them, he gets another chance."

Sometimes you will have to admit you are wrong in the face of your spouse's criticism, and this is never easy. It also can be tricky. Be sure not to play the "I know it's all my fault" game with your mate. It's easy to use that line as a means of manipulating your mate to feel apologetic and say in return, "Well, I suppose it's partially my fault, too."

When you face your spouse's criticism and know it's correct, keep these proverbs in mind:

If you refuse criticism you will end in poverty and disgrace; if you accept criticism you are on the road to fame (Prov. 13:18, *TLB*).

Don't refuse to accept criticism; get all the help you can (Prov. 23:12, *TLB*).

It is a badge of honor to accept valid criticism (Prov. 25:12, *TLB*).

If you're really at fault, then be willing to admit it. Say something like, "You know, I do think I'm to blame here. I'm sorry for what I said and I'm sorry that I hurt you. What can I do to help or make up for it?"

Let's back up for just a moment and look at the steps leading up to admitting you are wrong. The first step is to consider the truth of the criticism.

## Evaluate the Criticism for Validity

I realize this step may be easier said than done. Looking for value in criticism may be like searching for a needle in a haystack. But you must ask yourself, "What can I learn from this experience? Is there a grain of truth to which I need to respond?" These questions will shift you from the position of the defendant in a relationship to that of an investigator.

However unfair your spouse's attack, disregard the negative statements. Give your partner permission to exaggerate. Eventually the exaggerated statements will blow away like chaff and only the truth will remain. Keep searching for the grain of truth and try to identify the real cause for your spouse's criticism.

## Clarify the Root Problem

Try to determine precisely what your spouse thinks you have done or not done. It's important that you understand the criticism from your spouse's point of view. Ask specific questions such as, "Will you please elaborate on the main point?" or "Can you give me a specific example?" Suppose your spouse says, "You're the most inconsiderate person in the world!" That's a broad, general statement. Challenge your spouse to identify specific ways you have acted inconsiderately. Ask for examples from your relationship. Keep digging until the root is exposed.

## Think About the Charge

At times, the process of investigating an accusation or criticism may overwhelm you with anger, confusion or frustration. In the rush of these emotions, your mind may pull a disappearing act and go blank. You need time to think before you respond. How can you do that?

First, let me warn you about how *not* to do it. Don't ask, "Can I take a minute to think about this?" You don't need anyone's permission to take time to think. And don't say, "Are you sure you're seeing this situation accurately?" This question gives your spouse the opportunity to make another value judgment on the issue and vests him or her with unneeded power.

It's better to say, "I'm going to take a few minutes to think this over," or "That's an interesting perspective. I need to think about it." Then ask yourself, *What is the main point here? What does he (or she) want to happen as a result of our discussion?* Sometimes it's helpful to clarify that point with your mate by asking, "What would you like to be different about me as a result of our discussion? I'm really interested in knowing."

## Respond Positively and Confidently

Once the central issue has been exposed, explain your actions without withering defensively under the attack. I think people who criticize others expect their victims to be defensive, even though these critics sometimes say, "I wish he (or she) wouldn't become so defensive when I make a suggestion" (their word for a critical demand!). Critical people say they want their spouses to be nondefensive, but they are often shaken to the core when someone stands up to the criticism. When you know that what has been said is right, agree with it and tell your spouse what you will do differently next time.

## Don't Talk Too Much

Excessive talking can drive some of us up the wall—especially if we tend to be sparse with our words. Some people tend to talk on and on or they repeat what they have said; some people do a combination of the two. Consider what the Word of God has to say about excessive talking:

> Those who are careful about what they say protect their lives, but whoever speaks without thinking will be ruined (Prov. 13:3, *NCV*).

> The smart person says very little, and one with understanding stays calm. Even fools seem to be wise if they keep quiet; if they don't speak, they appear to understand (Prov. 17:27,28, *NCV*).

Some

counselors

suggest that

during a

difficult

discussion

you both

use no more

than 10 words

each time

you say

something.

Fools do not want to understand anything. They only want to tell others what they think (Prov. 18:2, *NCV*).

Those who are careful about what they say keep themselves out of trouble (Prov. 21:23, *NCV*).

Enough said? There is a time to speak and a time to be silent. Some personality types have a tendency to talk more than others. They are what we call *expanders*. They give an elaborate amount of detail when they talk. This is all right when talking with others who use the same style. But if an expander is in conversation with a *condenser*—someone who is spare with words—the condenser could become overwhelmed.

Sometimes the need-to-know principle should come into play, especially with people who tend to give information that isn't pertinent to what is being discussed. When the person you're talking to doesn't need all the information or isn't interested, give them the bottom line. They want the *Reader's Digest* condensed version, not the whole novel! Some counselors suggest that during a difficult discussion you each should use no more than 10 (that's right, 10) words each time you say something. Why not give it a try?

## What Do You Think?

1. Are you a condenser or an expander? Are you this way with everyone or do you make an exception with some people?
2. Which Scripture in this last section, if applied to your life, would help your relationship with your spouse?

## Silence Is Not Always Golden

Some people take the principle of not talking too much to the extreme and hardly say anything at all. In fact, they feel justified in using the silent treatment. There are numerous reasons for this response.

Some people use silence as a means of avoiding controversy or as a weapon to control, frustrate or manipulate. Sometimes a husband or wife takes the pathway of silence because it seems to be the least painful: perhaps one spouse is not a ready listener, or a spouse has been hurt so deeply that it keeps him or her silent.

Here is the typical pattern that results in the use of silence: When married partners are not communicating because one of them is silent, both of them experience frustration and a rising sense of futility, both of which compound the silence problem. The more the communicative person tries to talk, the farther the silent person draws into his or her shell. The communicator feels increasingly useless, inadequate and wounded and may try shouting or even acting violently in an attempt

Some people use silence to avoid controversy or as a weapon to control, frustrate or manipulate. When silence prevails, there is little opportunity to resolve issues and move forward in a relationship.

to get the silent mate to talk. This is futile because it does nothing more than drive the silent spouse into deeper silence. When you say to a silent person, "Why don't you talk to me?" or "Please say something; why can't we communicate?" or speak similar pleas, it usually does nothing more than reinforce that person's silence!

Silence can communicate a multitude of things: happiness, satisfaction, a sense of contentment and well-being. But more often than not it communicates dissatisfaction, contempt, anger, pouting, sulking and attitudes that say "Who gives a darn?" or "I'll show you." When silence prevails, there is little opportunity to resolve issues and move forward in a relationship. "Talk to me," we beg, and our spouse gets angry or continues to withdraw through silence. Too many of us use silence as a weapon.

Here are some questions and comments that may be effective ways of responding to silence: "What do you think about the question I asked you?" or "Your silence is telling me something; what are you trying to communicate by it?" or "I'd like to talk to you about your silence and what it does to me. But first I'd like to hear what you think about your silence."

Another approach might be to say, "I've noticed there are times when it's difficult for you to talk to me. Is there something I'm doing that makes it so hard to share with me that you'd rather be silent?" If your spouse responds with an answer, just let him or her talk. Don't attempt to defend yourself. Thank your spouse for sharing with you. If your spouse has not told you what he or she wants you to do differently, ask for a suggestion.

In the long run, silence never pays off. Even though the saying goes, "Silence is golden," it can also be yellow! Don't hide behind silence because you're afraid to deal with an issue.

## Avoid Nagging and Its Variations

"Nag"—doesn't that word have a nice tonal ring to it? It can bring misery to a relationship. Some have said that constant nagging can turn daily living into torture. That's a strong statement, but nagging is a destructive and unfair communication technique. Have you ever heard anyone say, "I enjoy nagging; in fact, I just love to nag"?

Let me clarify one point. Reminding is not the same as nagging. Most reminders are friendly. Nagging isn't. Reminders (for the most part) are usually accepted. Nagging isn't. The dictionary states that nagging is a persistent critical faultfinding response that creates a sense of irritation in the one being nagged. Nagging is often identified by the tone of voice. It often involves exaggeration as well. When you use words like "never," "always" or "all the time," the other person will cite the exceptions and become defensive. The truths hidden in your nagging will not be heard.

Some people say that the only time they get a response from their partner is when they nag, so it must work. Could it be they have trained or conditioned the partner over the years not to respond until the voice hits a certain octave and intensity? Do you sometimes try to talk to your spouse . . .

- while he or she is in another room? (You have no idea what your spouse is doing.)
- while you are on the run doing two or three things? (Which activity are you talking about?)
- while he or she is watching TV? (If it's sports, good luck!)
- while doing all of the above? (This is a disaster!)

It helps if you . . .

- make sure your spouse isn't involved with something that prevents him or her from connecting with you.
- stop what you're doing and go to where your spouse is.
- look your spouse in the eye while speaking slowly, softly and pleasantly, with your hand resting gently on his or her shoulder; you'll be amazed at the difference in his or her response.

When you make a request, never accept the answer "I'll do it later" until you define what is meant by the word "later." You may think later means in two hours, while the other person is thinking two days!

Sometimes we invite nagging. A man came in for counseling and said, "Our marriage is actually quite good except for one problem. My wife tends to nag me from time to time!"

I asked what he meant by nag.

"Well, three times in the last week she asked if I was going to clean out the garage. That's what."

My response was that it sounded more like reminding than nagging.

He said, "Nagging or reminding—I don't care which it is. I just want her to stop!"

At this point, I decided to join him rather than debate him, and said, "You know, I agree with you. I think it would be a good idea if she stopped. And I think I've got an idea on how to get her to do that."

His eyes opened wide. "You do?"

"Yes, I do. It's simple. If you have given any indication that you would clean out the garage, just follow through with your commitment and your wife won't feel compelled to call you back to it."

He didn't like what I said for one good reason—that's exactly what had happened. He said he would clean the garage and then didn't do it. Anytime we're being reminded (or nagged), is there something we have or haven't done that may be contributing to the reminder? It's something to consider.

I heard the story of a wife who would ask her husband to fix something around the house and he would agree to do it. Unfortunately, he would keep postponing the task, but he didn't want anyone else to do it. He wanted to save the money involved in hiring someone and also felt he could do a better job. Because nothing was happening, the wife's reminders had turned into nagging.

The couple went to a counselor who suggested that when the wife noticed something that needed to be repaired, she would ask her husband to do it. If he agreed, they put it on the calendar. He had 15 days in which to fix the needed repair, during which time she couldn't say a word. If the husband hadn't fixed it by the end of 15 days, the wife could call in a repairman and the husband would pay the bill without saying a word. The agreement was made and only once did she have to call a repairman.

There is a principle here that is applicable to any area of marriage: If what you're doing isn't working, why keep doing it? There's got to be a better way! Find it and do it![1]

Scripture tells us:

Don't talk so much. You keep putting your foot in your mouth. Be sensible and turn off the flow! (Prov. 10:19, *TLB*).

Pleasant words are as a honeycomb, sweet to the mind and healing to the body (Prov. 16:24, *AMP*).

He who covers over an offense promotes love, but whoever repeats the matter separates close friends (Prov.
17:9, *NIV*).

It is better to dwell in a corner of the housetop [on
the flat oriental roof, exposed to all kinds of weath-
er] than in a house shared with a nagging, quarrelsome, and faultfinding woman (Prov. 21:9, *AMP*).

(By the way, both men and women are capable of nagging.)

Patrick Morley has given us a choice thought about our
communication as husbands and wives:

Words are the window into the soul. Words escort my
mate into my inner being, and usher me into her inner-
most thoughts. Words give form and expression to our
deepest thoughts. Words are valuable.

We use words to paint the portrait of our love for each
other. "I love the way you do your hair." A few sincere
words skillfully clumped together can lift the spirit of
your partner high into the heavens. Words are beautiful.

Words capture the raw intensity of our passion.
Mark Twain said, "A powerful agent is the right word."
Words can be like the pressure valve on a steam cooker
that lets off steam. Or the arrow through the bull's-eye
that heals a wounded mate. Words are powerful.

Sometimes, though, words don't come. We cannot
find the words to express our deepest feelings. Language
can be inadequate to get across our meaning. Sometimes
the right word eludes us altogether. Other times, it teases

us by buzzing around our head, never landing long enough to be captured. And sometimes, the word that comes just doesn't measure up to the beauty of the feeling. Mark Twain also said, "The difference between the right word and the almost right word is the difference between lightning and the lightning bug." Words can be inadequate.

It is the duty of every husband and wife to know the times they should speak words of encouragement, comfort, challenge and inspiration to their spouses. We have responsibility for each other's nurturing. It is likewise the duty of every husband and wife to know when to remain silent. There are times of silence when the highest form of love we can express may be a hand laid gently on our mate's hand or shoulder.

Never leave a thought or feeling left unsaid that may build up and encourage your mate. It is the ministry of words. Conversely, never say something better left unsaid. There is a time for everything.[2]

## What Do You Think?

1. List five things you have asked (or nagged) your mate about that he or she has not changed or improved one bit. Why do you want your mate to change in these areas? Would the changes bring his or her behavior or attitude into closer harmony with Scripture? How else could you get your mate to change rather than to keep mentioning it (nagging)?

2. List five things your mate has asked (or nagged) you about but you have not changed, either because you could not or did not wish to do so.

3. Of the items listed for question 2, which ones could you have corrected if you had really wanted to do so?

There are two other guidelines from the Word of God. First, *Don't respond in anger; it's best to use a kind response* (see Prov. 14:29; 15:1; 25:15; 29:11; Eph. 4:26,31. And the other, which will be addressed at length in the next chapter: *Listen to your spouse* (see Prov. 18:13; Jas. 1:19).

God's Word gives us the effective guidelines to follow. There are additional principles, which we'll look at as well. But for any of these guidelines and principles it all comes down to three things—following them, applying them and praying that the Holy Spirit will assist you in recalling and following them.

That's everyone's responsibility.

## What's Your Plan?

1. Sit down with your marriage partner and talk over the principles discussed in this chapter. Make a mutual commitment to try to follow them in the future. Agree to be accountable to one another and devise a plan for regular evaluation of how well you are succeeding.
2. If either one of you violates any of the principles, how will you handle the violation? List ideas for a procedure that both of you will be able to accept and carry out.

*Notes*
1. Sven Wahlroos, *Family Communication* (New York: Macmillan, 1974), pp. 189-205, adapted.
2. Patrick Morley, *Two-Part Harmony* (Nashville, Tenn.: Thomas Nelson, 1994), pp. 60, 61.

# THE GIFT OF LISTENING

CHAPTER SIX

One of the greatest gifts one person can give to another is the gift of listening. It can be an act of love and caring. But far too many couples only *hear* one another. Few actually *listen*.

One person said that if we could listen to all the conversations of the world between married couples, we would see that for the most part they are dialogues of the deaf.

Do you know what it is to have someone listen to you—not just hear you, but really listen to you? Look at these verses from the Word of God that tell us how God listens to us:

The eyes of the LORD are toward the righteous, and His ears are open to their cry. The face of the LORD is against evildoers, to cut off the memory of them from the earth. The righteous cry and the LORD hears, and delivers them out of all their troubles. The LORD is near to the brokenhearted, and saves those who are crushed in spirit (Ps. 34:15-18).

I love the LORD, because He hears my voice and my supplications. Because He has inclined His ear to me, therefore I shall call upon Him as long as I live (Ps. 116:1,2).

He who gives an answer before he hears, it is folly and shame to him (Prov. 18:13).

Any story sounds true until someone tells the other side and sets the record straight (Prov. 18:17, *TLB*).

The wise man learns by listening; the simpleton can learn only by seeing scorners punished (Prov. 21:11, *TLB*).

Call to Me, and I will answer you, and I will tell you great and mighty things, which you do not know (Jer. 33:3).

Let every man be quick to hear [a ready listener] (Jas. 1:19, *AMP*).

What do we mean by listening? What do we mean by hearing? Is there a difference? Hearing involves gaining content or information for your own purposes. Listening involves caring for and being empathic toward the person who is talking. Hearing means that you are concerned about what is going on inside *you* during the conversation. Listening means that you are trying to understand the feelings of *the other person* and are listening for his or her sake.

Let me give you a threefold definition of listening when it pertains to your spouse talking to you:

1. Listening means that you're not thinking about what you're going to say when he or she stops talking. You

are not busy formulating your response. You're concentrating on what is being said and you're putting into practice Proverbs 18:13 (*NIV*): "He who answers before listening—that is his folly and his shame."

2. Listening means that you're completely accepting of what is being said, without judging what the person is saying or how he or she is saying it. If you don't like your spouse's tone of voice or the words used and you react on the spot, you may miss the meaning. Perhaps your spouse hasn't said it in the best way, but why not listen and then come back later—when both of you are calm—to discuss the proper wording and tone of voice? Acceptance doesn't mean that you agree with the content of what your spouse says. It means that you acknowledge and understand that what your spouse is saying is something he or she is feeling.

3. Listening means being able to repeat what your spouse has said and express what you think he or she was feeling while speaking to you. Real listening implies having an interest in your spouse's feelings and opinions and attempting to understand those feelings from his or her perspective.

"Listening is a sharp attention to what is going on. It is an active openness toward your spouse. Listening is putting your whole self in a position to respond to whatever he or she cares to say."[1] Listening to your spouse means letting go of your concerns, wants and investment in your own position long enough to consider the other person. When you are doing the talking, you're not usually learning. But you learn when you listen.

Listening is a learnable skill. Your mind and ears can be taught to hear more keenly; your eyes can be taught to see more

Real listening
implies an
interest in
your spouse's
feelings and
opinions
and an
attempt to
understand
those feelings
from his
or her
perspective.

clearly. You can also learn to *hear* with your eyes and *see* with your ears. Jesus said: "Therefore I speak to them in parables; because while seeing they do not see, and while hearing they do not hear, nor do they understand. And in their case, the prophecy of Isaiah is being fulfilled, which says, 'You will keep on hearing, but will not understand; and you will keep on seeing, but will not perceive; for the heart of this people has become dull, and with their ears they scarcely hear, and they have closed their eyes lest they could see with their eyes, and hear with their ears, and understand with their heart and return, and I should heal them'" (Matt. 13:13-15).

Let your ears hear and see.

Let your eyes see and hear.

The word "hear" in the New Testament does not usually refer to an auditory experience. It usually means to pay heed. As you listen to your spouse you need to pay heed to what he or she is saying. It requires tuning into the right frequency.

If you listen, you adventure
in the lives of other people.
We soon notice the people

who really take us seriously and listen to what we have to say. And with them we tend to open more of our lives than with the busy nonlistener. We share what really matters. Thus, if you are such a listener, the chances are good that others will invite you as a guest into their lives. Because they know you will hear them, they will entrust you with things that mean very much to them. And this, too, is more rewarding![2]

Because of my retarded son, Matthew, who did not have a vocabulary, I learned to listen with my eyes. I learned to read the message in his nonverbal signals. This translated to my listening to what my counselees could not put into words. I learned to listen to the message behind the message—the hurt, the ache, the frustration, the loss of hope, the fear of rejection, the feeling of betrayal, the joy, the delight, the promise of change. I also learned to reflect upon what I see on a client's face and in his posture, walk and pace. Then I tell him what I see. This provides the counselee an opportunity to explain further what he's thinking and feeling. He *knows* I'm tuned in to him.

## The Ways We Communicate

Every message has three components: (1) the actual content, (2) the tone of voice and (3) the nonverbal communication. It is possible to use the same word, statement or question and express many different messages simply by changing tone of voice or body movement. Nonverbal communication includes facial expression, body posture and gestures or actions.

The three components of communication must be complementary in order for a simple message to be transmitted. It has been suggested that successful communication consists of 7-percent content, 38-percent tone of voice and 55-percent nonverbal communication. We're usually aware of the content of what we're saying but not nearly as aware of our tone of voice. We have the capability of giving one sentence a dozen different meanings just by changing our tone. Tape record some of your dinner conversations sometime and then sit down and listen to yourself. You'll be amazed.

When a man says to his wife, with the proper tone of voice, "Dear, I love you," but he buries his head in a newspaper, what is she to believe? When a woman asks, "How was your day?" in a flat tone, while passing her husband on the way to another room, what does he respond to—the verbal or nonverbal message?

A husband, as he leaves for work, comes up to his wife, smiles, gives her a hug and a kiss and states in a loving voice, "I really love you." After he leaves, she really feels good. But when she notices the newspaper in the middle of the room, pajamas on the bed, dirty socks on the floor and the toothpaste tube with the cap off lying in the sink, her good feeling begins to dissipate. She has told her husband how important it is to her that he assume responsibility for cleaning up after himself. But he has been careless again. She believed his statement of love when he left for work, but now she wonders, *If he really meant what he said, why doesn't he show it by assuming some responsibility? I wonder if he really does love me.* His earlier actions contradicted his message of love, even though the message may have been sent properly.

Concerning nonverbal communication, Dr. Mark Lee writes:

Marital problems may grow out of unsatisfactory nonverbal communications. Vocal variables are important carriers of meaning. We interpret the sound of a voice, both consciously and subconsciously. We usually can tell the emotional meanings of the speaker by voice pitch, rate of speech, loudness, and voice quality. We can tell the sincerity or insincerity, the conviction or lack of conviction, the truth or falsity of most statements we hear. When a voice is raised in volume and pitch, the words will not convey the same meaning as when spoken softly in a lower register. The high, loud voice, with rapid rate and harsh quality, will likely communicate a degree of emotion that will greatly obscure the verbal message. The nonverbal manner in which a message is delivered is registered most readily by the listener. It may or may not be remembered for recall. However, the communicator tends to recall what he said rather than the manner of his speech.[3]

## The Ways We Listen

There are many types of listening. Some people listen for facts, information and details for their own use. Others listen because they feel sorry for the person. Some people listen to gossip because they revel in the juicy story of another person's failures or difficulties. On occasion, people listen out of obligation, out of necessity or to be polite. Some who listen are nothing more than voyeurs who have an incessant need to pry and probe into other people's lives.

Some people listen because they care. Sensitive listening and hearing are open mine shafts to intimacy. But all too often the potential for listening lies untapped within us like a load of unmined gold because of barriers that inhibit our listening.

Why do you listen? What are your motives? Any or all of the above? Listening that springs from caring builds closeness, reflects love and is an act of grace.

# What Do You Think?

1. Describe your tone of voice when you are upset. How would your spouse describe it?
2. What are some of your positive nonverbals? What are some negative ones?
3. What are some of your spouse's positive nonverbals? What are some negative ones?
4. What tone of voice and what nonverbals would help the communication in your marriage?

Are you aware that a listener, not the speaker, controls the conversation? Probably not, since most of us operate under the myth that the more we talk, the more we influence the listener. If both people in a conversation believe this, the talking escalates and becomes more intense, making words fly through the air with nowhere to land. Deafness prevails!

What do I mean by saying the listener controls the conversation? Compare listening to the driving a car. The person talking can be likened to the engine; the person listening can be likened to the person at the wheel. The engine provides the power, but the person at the wheel has the power to decide where the car will go. You, the listener, can give direction and guide the flow of the conversation by the statements you make and the questions you ask.

This is what is called *paraphrasing*. When you paraphrase what another person is saying, that person will continue to talk. And when you verbally agree with the talker, you cause the person to share even more.

I've heard people say, "When I listen, it seems to cause the other person to just talk and talk and talk. Why?" Perhaps initially it does, but if you remain perfectly silent, you create such tension within the person speaking that he or she begins to back off. I'm not talking about using the silent treatment—that devastatingly unfair weapon that in time will erode a relationship. But by not responding, you let the other individual know that you are through with your part of the conversation, and your silence points to the fact that true communication is a give-and-take process.

Why do we listen to other people? Partly because we've been taught or admonished to do so. But there are four basic reasons why we listen to other people:

1. To understand the other person
2. To enjoy the other person
3. To learn something from the one talking (such as learning his or her language)
4. To give help, assistance or comfort to the person

The world is made up of many pseudolisteners who masquerade as the real product. But anyone who has not listened for the above reasons does not really listen.

## Barriers to Listening

In order for caring listening to occur, we need to be aware of some of the common obstacles to communication. I have identified nine possible obstacles to listening.

### Defensiveness

We miss the message if our minds are busy thinking up a rebuttal, excuse or exception to what our spouse is saying.

There are a variety of defensive responses. *Perhaps we reach a premature conclusion.* "All right, I know just what you're going to say. We've been through this before and it's the same old thing."

*We may read into our spouse's words our own expectations or project onto him or her what we would say in the same situation.* David Augsburger writes:

> Prejudging a communication as uninteresting or unimportant lifts the burden of listening off one's shoulders and frees the attention to wander elsewhere. But two persons are being cheated: the other is not being given a fair hearing, and the listener is being deprived of what may be useful information. I want to cancel all advance judgments—prejudgments—and recognize them for what they are, prejudices. I want to hear the other in a fresh, new way with whatever energies I have available.[4]

Two other defensive indicators may be: *rehearsing our responses* and *responding to explosive words.*

Rehearsing a response (as well as other defensive postures) is not what the Scriptures call us to do as listeners. "He who answers a matter before he hears the facts, it is folly and shame to him" (Prov. 18:13, *AMP*).

Explosive words create an inner explosion of emotions. Explosive words include phrases such as: "That's crude"; "That's just like a woman (or man)"; "You're *always* late"; "You *never* ask me what I think"; "You're becoming just like your mother." Not only do we react to explosive words, but we also may consciously choose to use some words that make it difficult for our spouses to listen. What are the words that set you off? What is your spouse's list of explosive words?

Not all defensiveness is overtly expressed. Outwardly we could be agreeing, but inside we're saying just the opposite. If your spouse confronts you about a behavior or attitude, do you accept the criticism or defend yourself?

## Personal Biases

We may have a biased attitude toward a person who speaks in a certain tone of voice, a person of a certain ethnic group, someone of the opposite sex, someone who reminds us of a person from our past and so on, which causes us to reject a person or a personality without listening to what the person has to say. In effect, we're saying, "If you are _____ (and I don't like people who are _____), I don't need to listen to you."

Our personal biases will affect how well we listen. For example, it may be easier to listen to an angry person than to a sarcastic person; some tones or phrases may be enjoyable to listen to, whereas others may be annoying; the repetitive phrases a person uses (and may be unaware of) can bother us; excessive gestures, such as talking with the hands or waving the arms, can be overly distracting.

Some people are distracted from listening because of the gender of the person speaking. They are influenced by their expectations of what is appropriate for a man to share or not share or for a woman to share or not share. Some people may listen more (or less) attentively to someone who is in a position over them, in a lesser position or simply in a prestigious position. The stereotypes we assign to people influence how we listen to them.

## Different Listening Styles

One person hears with optimism and another with pessimism. I hear the bad news and you hear the good news. If your spouse shares a frustrating and difficult situation with you, you may stop listening because you view it as complaining. Or you may listen more closely because you view it as an act of trust in you.

Lack of understanding of gender differences in listening and conversation creates problems. Women use more verbal responses to *encourage* the talker. They're more likely than men to use listening signals like "mm-hmmm" and "yeah" just to indicate they are listening.

A man will use this response only when he's *agreeing* with what his wife is saying. You can see what the outcome could be! A husband interprets his wife's listening responses as signs that she agrees with him. He's thinking, *All right! Good deal! We can buy that new sports car!* Later on, he discovers she wasn't agreeing with him at all. He didn't realize she was simply indicating her interest in what he was saying and in keeping the interchange going. His wife, on the other hand, may feel ignored and disappointed because he doesn't make the same listening responses she does. She interprets his quietness as not caring.

A man is more likely than a woman to make comments throughout the conversation. But a woman may feel bothered after she's been interrupted or hasn't been given any listening feedback. This is why many wives complain "My husband always interrupts me" or "He never listens to me."

When it comes to a man's communication style, here is a recap of some things to keep in mind:

- He is more likely to interrupt the other person, whether the person is male or female.
- He is less likely to respond to the comments of the other person and, many times, makes no response at all, gives a delayed response after the person's statement or

shows a minimum degree of enthusiasm.

- He is more likely to challenge or dispute statements made by his partner, which explains why a husband may seem to be argumentative.
- He tends to make more statements of fact or opinion than a woman does.

Given the contrast between the listening and talking styles of men and women, it's easy to see why misunderstandings arise. A wife might easily perceive her husband as uninterested or unresponsive. That may not be the case; it's just his way of responding to everyone, not just to her. If a wife says "He never listens to me" or "He disagrees with everything I say," it's probably more a reflection of his communication style than insensitivity.

Understanding and accepting these differences can help you accept your spouse's style without taking offense. This is one of the first steps of what we call *gender-flex*—understanding the differences and making it a point to adapt and

Given the contrast between the listening and talking styles of men and women, it's easy to see why misunderstandings arise.

even use the other gender's style in order to bridge the differences (this concept will be expanded later).[5]

## Inner Struggles

We have difficulty listening when our emotional involvement
reaches the point where we are unable to separate ourselves from
the other person. You may find it easier to listen to the problems
of other people than to your spouse's because of your emotional involvement. Listening may also be difficult if you blame
yourself for your spouse's difficulties.

What someone says may cause threatening feelings to surface. Our listening can be hindered if we're fearful that our own
emotions may become activated. A man can feel extremely ill at
ease as his emotions surge to the surface. Can you think of a
time when you listened to another person and felt so overwhelmed with feelings that you were unable to hear what the
person was saying?

We may feel hindered in listening to someone if the person
has certain expectations of us. If we dislike the other person, we
probably won't listen to him very well. And if someone speaks
too loudly or too softly, we may struggle to keep listening.

## The Habit of Interrupting

When we feel like the other person isn't getting to the point fast
enough, we may start asking for information that would be
forthcoming anyway. Have you ever found yourself saying,
"Hold it. I've got a dozen ideas cooking because of what you said.
Let me tell you some of them . . ."? It's easy for our minds to wander, for we think at five times the rate we speak. If a person
speaks at 100 words a minute and you're listening at the rate of

500 per minute, what do you do? Even though you process information faster than it can be verbalized, you can choose either to stay in pace with the speaker or to let your mind wander.

## Mental Overload

Perhaps someone comes along with yet another new piece of information and you just can't handle it. You feel bombarded from all sides and don't have enough time to digest what you already know. Your mind feels like a juggler with too many items to juggle, thus it becomes difficult to listen to anything.

## Bad Timing

Have you ever heard comments such as: "Talk? Now? At 2:30 in the morning?" "Just a minute. There's only 35 seconds left in the final quarter of the game." "I'd like to listen but I'm already late for an appointment." Choosing the right time to speak can be crucial to the listening process.

## Physical Exhaustion

Both mental and physical fatigue make it difficult to listen. There are times when you need to let your partner know that right then isn't a good time, but be sure to tell your partner when you will be able to listen.

## Selective Attention

Another way of expressing this obstacle is filtered listening—screening the information being shared. If we have a negative attitude, we may ignore, distort or reject positive messages. Often we hear what we want to hear or what fits in with our mind-set. If we engage in selective listening, we probably engage in selective retention. That means we remember only certain comments and situations. David Augsburger describes the process this way:

> Memory is the greatest editor of all, and it discards major pieces of information while treasuring trifles. When I try to work through an unresolved conflict that is only an hour old, I find my memory—which I present as though it were complete, perfect and unretouched—is quite different from my partner's—which I can see is partial, biased and clearly rewritten. We both have selective memories.
>
> Selectivity is an asset. It saves us from being overloaded with stimuli, overwhelmed with information, overtaxed with demands from a humming, buzzing environment.
>
> Selectivity is also a liability. If I deny that it is taking place there will be much that I don't see, and I won't see that I don't see. If I pretend I saw it all, understood it all, recall it all, there will be many times when I will argue in vain or cause intense pain in relationship with my inability to hear the other person whose point of view is equally good, although probably as partial as my own. We each—even at our best—see in part, understand only in part, and recall only a small part.[6]

## What Do You Think?

1. Of the nine obstacles to listening that were listed, which three will you select to work on this week?

2. Which three would your spouse like you to work on?
3. Discuss your lists to discover how you can assist one another.

## Overcoming Obstacles to Listening

Do you know what hinders you from listening? Who is responsible for the obstacle—your partner or you?

The initial step to overcoming an obstacle is to identify it. Of those obstacles listed, which one do you identify as yours? Who controls this barrier, you or the one speaking? Perhaps you can rearrange the situation or the conditions so that listening becomes easier. You may need to discuss what each of you can do to become a better listener.

### Understand What You Feel About Your Spouse

How you view your spouse affects how you listen to him or her. A partner's communication is colored by how you view him. This view may have been shaped by your observations of his past performance or by your own defensiveness.

### Listen with Your Whole Body

If your partner asks, "Are you listening to me?" and you say "Yes," while walking away or fixing dinner or doing the dishes, perhaps you aren't really listening. Concentrate on the person and the message. Give your undivided attention. Turn off the appliance or the TV when there is an important matter to talk about; set aside what you're doing and listen.

There are several responses you can use to indicate you are catching all of what your spouse is saying.

1. *Clarifying.* This response reflects on the true meaning and intention of what has been said. "I think what you're saying is that you trust me to keep my promise to you, but you're still a bit concerned about my being away just before your birthday."

2. *Observing.* This response focuses upon the nonverbal or tonal quality of what your partner has said. "I noticed that your voice was dropping when you talked about your job."

3. *Reflective listening.* A reflective statement attempts to pick up the feelings that have been expressed. Usually a feeling word is included in the response, such as, "You seem quite sad (joyful, happy, delighted, angry) about that."

4. *Inquiring.* An inquiry draws out more information about the meaning of what was said. A very simple response would be, "I would like you to tell me more."

## Be Patient

If your spouse is a slow or hesitant talker, you may have a tendency to jump in whenever you find an opening and finish a statement or hurry your spouse along. You can't assume that you really know what is going to be said. You can't read your partner's mind.

David Augsburger, in his book *Caring Enough to Hear,* lists 10 commandments for better listening. These commandments are a good recap of all the principles we have discussed in this chapter.

I. *On passing judgment.* Thou shalt neither judge nor evaluate until thou hast truly understood. ("Hold it right there, I've heard enough to know where you stand, and you're all wet.")

II. *On adding insights.* Thou shalt not attribute ideas or contribute insights to those stated. ("If you mean this, it will lead to there, and then you must also mean that.")

III. *On assuming agreement.* Thou shalt not assume that what you heard is what was truly said or what was really meant. ("I know what you meant, no matter what you say now. I heard you with my own ears.")

IV. *On drifting attention.* Thou shalt not permit thy thoughts to stray or thy attention to wander. ("When you said that, it triggered an interesting idea that I like better than yours.")

V. *On closing the mind.* Thou shalt not close thy mind to opposing thoughts, thy ears to opposite truths, thy eyes to other views. ("After you used that sexist language, I didn't hear another thing you said.")

VI. *On wishful hearing.* Thou shalt not permit thy heart to rule thy mind, nor thy mind thy heart. ("I just knew you were going to say that; I had it figured all along.")

VII. *On multiple meanings.* Thou shalt not interpret words except as they are interpreted by the speaker. ("If I were to stop breathing, would I or would I not expire?")

VIII. *On rehearsing responses.* Thou shalt not use the other person's time to prepare responses of your own. ("I can't wait until you need a breath. Have I got a come-back for you!")

IX. *On fearing challenge.* Thou shalt not fear correction, improvement or change. ("I'm talking faster to snow you because I don't want to hear what you've got to say.")

X. *On evading equality.* Thou shalt not overdemand time or fail to claim your own time to hear and be heard. ("I want equal time. I want you to feel equally heard.")[7]

Above all, listen to your spouse in an attitude of love. When you listen in love, you are able to wait for the other person to share the meaning of his or her thoughts and feelings.

## What's Your Plan?

1. List three steps you will take to enhance your listening ability.
2. What topic would you like your spouse to listen to with full attention?

*Notes*
1. George E. Koehler and Nikki Koehler, *My Family: How Shall I Live with It?* (Chicago: Rand McNally & Company, 1968), p. 57, adapted.
2. Ibid., p. 62.

3. Mark Lee, *Make More of Your Marriage,* ed. Gary Collins (Waco, Tex.: Word Books, 1976), p. 75.
4. David Augsburger, *Caring Enough to Hear* (Ventura, Calif.: Regal Books, 1982), p. 46.
5. Aaron T. Beck, *Love Is Never Enough* (New York: Harper & Row, 1988), pp. 74-81, adapted.
6. Augsburger, *Caring Enough to Hear,* pp. 41, 42.
7. Ibid., pp. 55-58.

# ARE MEN REALLY FROM PLUTO AND WOMEN FROM SATURN?

CHAPTER SEVEN

Many years ago most of us learned to drive a car. Many, many years ago most people learned on stick shifts primarily because few cars had automatic transmissions. The gearshift was on the steering column or it was on the floor. It was tricky to learn to coordinate pushing the clutch as you shifted from one gear to the next. If you did it right, it went smoothly and quietly. If not, you ground the gears. You could hear as well as feel the metal clashing and grinding. If you did this often enough you would grind the gears into fine pieces of metal, eventually ruining the transmission.

The same thing can happen to two people attempting to become compatible. You can end up grinding and clashing against one another. Aside from the previously discussed areas in which meshing needs to occur, such as the way we communicate with each other, another major issue comes into play when you seek to learn each other's culture—the blending of gender and personality differences. This meshing or blending is a major step in learning to speak your spouse's language.

Too often we hear gender differences reduced to one factor, such as personality preferences or being left- or right-brained. It actually makes more sense to look at men and women as complex mixtures of differences.

Understanding and adapting to a partner's personality, which includes gender uniqueness as well as brain dominance and personality, will make the difference as to whether or not they adjust to this foreigner! When a man and woman are in sync, the gears don't grind as they shift in a close relationship, and the communication between the two is positive. To make this smooth shifting happen, couples need to accept two facts:

1. Men and women are wired differently. Neither is wired incorrectly, just differently.
2. For a relationship to blossom, men and women need to become bilingual, each fluent in the language of the opposite sex.

Several years ago my wife and I had an experience that dramatically portrayed gender differences in both thought and communication styles. We were visiting historical Williamsburg in Virginia, a fascinating and charming setting that preserves our colonial history. When we took the tour of the governor's mansion, the tour guide was a man. As we entered the large entry door, he began to give a factual description of the purpose of the room as well as the way it was furnished. He described in detail the various ancient guns on the wall and pointed to the unique display of flintlock rifles arranged in a circle on the rounded ceiling. When he said there were 64 of them, some originals and others replicas, I immediately began counting them (which is a typical male response—we're into numbers). The guide was knowledgeable and he gave an excellent detailed description as we went from room to room. He seemed to be quite structured and focused.

We had to leave before the tour was completed to meet some friends for lunch. Because we both enjoyed the presentation so much, we decided to return the next day and take the tour again. What a difference! The guide was a woman. We entered the same room and she said, "Now you'll notice a few guns on the wall and ceiling, but notice the covering on these chairs and the tapestry on the walls. They are . . ." And with that she launched into a detailed description of items that had either been ignored or just given a passing mention the day before. And on it went throughout the tour.

It didn't take much to figure out what was going on. It was a classic example of gender differences. The first tour guide was speaking more to men and the second guide was speaking more to women. Actually, we ended up with the best tour imaginable because we heard both perspectives. What a benefit it would be to the tourists if the guides incorporated both perspectives into their presentations!

## Gender Views About Communication

We've asked men and women in a seminar setting to identify what frustrates them about the communication style of the opposite sex. Here's a listing of some of their responses:

## What Women Said About Men

They don't share their feelings or emotions enough. It's like they grew up emotionally handicapped.

They seem to go into a trance when they're watching sports or when I bring up certain subjects. They're not able to handle more than one task or subject at a time.

Men seem to think they can do things better, even when they can't. And they won't take any advice, even if it helps them.

They don't listen well. They're always trying to fix our problems.

Men need more intuition—get off the factual bandwagon.

Men need to learn to enjoy shopping like we do. They just don't know what they're missing.

Men need more sensitivity, concern, compassion and empathy.

I wish men weren't so threatened by women's ideas and perspectives.

They're so overinvolved in their work and career. They want a family but they don't get involved.

Sex—that's the key word. Don't they think about anything else? They're like a microwave oven. Push the button and they're cookin'. Their On button is never off.

Here are some other responses that were recorded in a group setting:

Men think too much. There's more to life than thinking.

I wish he didn't think he always had to define everything. I feel as if I've been talking to a dictionary. Every week for the past year my husband has said, "What do you mean? I can't talk to you if I don't understand your words. Give me some facts, not those darn feelings!" Well, sometimes I can't give him facts and definitions. Man shall not live by definitions alone!

I don't think men understand the difference between sharing their feelings and what they think about their feelings. They tend to intellectualize so much of the time. Why do men have to think about how they feel? Just come out with it unedited. He doesn't have to respond like a textbook or edit everything he shares. I wonder if the emotional side of a man threatens him? Of course you can't always control your emotional responses. So what?

My husband is an engineer and you ought to be around when his engineer friends come over. The house is like a cerebral, cognitive conference! All logical facts. They walk in with their slide rulers and calculators, and it's as though the house were swept clean of any emotional response. They talk, but they don't disclose. They share, but on the surface. They're safe and secure. Sometimes I have this urge to come into the room and start sharing emotions with all sorts of emotional words, and then start crying and see how long it would take for some of them to bolt out the door, jump out the window or hide their faces behind a magazine. Why, I could even threaten 10 men inside of a minute. I never realized what power I had. I think I'll do that next time they're over.

What about men? What frustrates them about women? It's generally the opposite of what women say frustrates them about men.

## What Men Said About Women

They're too emotional. They need to be more logical.

How can they spend so much time talking? When it's said, it's said. So many of them are expanders. I wish they would get to the bottom line quicker and at least identify the subject!

They're too sensitive. They're always getting their feelings hurt.

Why do they cry so easily? It doesn't make sense to me.

I think most women are shopaholics. Their eyes glaze over when they see a shopping mall.

They're so changeable. I wish they'd make up their minds and then keep them made up.

Maybe they think we can read minds, but we can't. I don't think they can either.

What's wrong with the sex drive? Sex is great, only they don't have that much interest. It takes forever to get them interested.

They think they have the spiritual gift of changing men. They ought to quit. We can't be fixed and we don't need to be.

They're so involved with other people and their problems.

Women are moody and negative. You can't satisfy them.

I wish they would leave some things alone. They're always trying to fix something that isn't broken.

Here are some additional responses men have shared in seminars:

I understand her need to talk about us and our relationship. I happen to think that there is a right and a wrong way to talk about those things. If you're not careful, the whole thing can get out of hand. It's best to be as rational as possible. If you let it get too emotional, you never can make any good decisions, and if it gets too personal, someone could get hurt. A little bit of distance goes a long way, where a lot of these things are concerned.

It's important, first, to set out clearly what the issues are. I don't think women do this very well. They latch on to the first thing that comes to mind, get totally emotionally involved in it. The next thing you know, you're arguing about everything under the sun, and no one is happy. I believe in a clear definition of the problem at the outset. If she can tell me exactly what is bothering her, we can deal with it logically. If she can't do that, then there's no sense even talking about it.

## What Do You Think?

1. Describe how you and your spouse differ in communication styles.
2. What frustrates you or concerns you about your spouse's communication style?
3. How do you wish your spouse would communicate differently?

## Not Wrong, Just Different

As we consider some of the unique characteristics of men and women, let's keep two things in mind. First, there are some generalizations that pertain to most men and women. But there will always be exceptions in varying degrees. Second, the characteristics unique to men and to women are not negative. It is not a fault to be either way. Some of the characteristics will be more pronounced in some people because of personality types as well as upbringing. The problem arises when people feel they are always right or that the way they do things is the only right way. They don't care about understanding and accepting the opposite sex the way they are. The more flexibility a person develops, the more his or her marriage will benefit.[1]

It's not easy to flex and learn to respond differently, but it's possible. You need to make a conscious effort to understand what is second nature to your partner and vice versa.

Many men and women say they know about the differences between the sexes, such as feeling versus fact, brain differences, energy levels and so on. But their interaction often leads to this question: If they know about the differences, why do they keep fighting something that is a natural and inherited ability, as well as a way of being that has been designed by God Himself?

If people really knew the differences between male and female styles of thinking and communicating, they would be able to explain the differences in detail and accept them. They would honor the differences and respond to each other in an appropriate and accepting way.

The following may seem like a basic course in biology, physiology and anthropology, but it really isn't. It's simply an explanation of some basic gender differences that most people still allow to confuse them and to dictate their responses to the opposite sex.

If people really knew the differences between male and female styles of thinking and communicating, they would honor the differences and respond to each other in an appropriate and accepting way.

Much of the mystery is solved when you understand the less-obvious physiological differences between men and women. When Scripture says that God created them male and female, He really did create us differently: "Now the Lord God said, It is not good (sufficient, satisfactory) that the man should be alone; I will make him a helper meet (suitable, adapted, complementary) for him" (Genesis 2:18, *AMP*). Much of these differences are found in the brain.

## How the Brain Functions

The left hemisphere controls language and reading skills. It gathers information and processes it logically in a step-by-step fashion. When is the left brain used? When you read a book or article, play a game, sing, write, balance your checkbook and weigh the advantages and disadvantages of buying an item on time versus paying cash.

If you're planning your day's schedule, you may decide to leave 10 minutes early to drop off the video you rented the night before, and you'll plan the route that will enable you to park in front of the store. How did you make these decisions? By using the left portion of your brain. It keeps your life sensible, organized and on schedule. It's like a computer.

And then we have the right side of the brain. That portion of your brain comes into play when you work a jigsaw puzzle, look at a road map, design a new office, plan a room arrangement, solve a geometrical problem or listen to musical selections on the stereo. The right half of your brain does not process information step-by-step like the left portion. Instead, it processes patterns of information. It plays host to our emotions. It has been called the intuitive side of the brain. It will link facts together and come up with a concept. It looks at the whole situation and, as though by magic, the solution appears. It's like a kaleidoscope.

The thinking pattern of the left side of your brain is analytical, linear, explicit, sequential, verbal, concrete, rational and goal oriented. The right side is spontaneous, intuitive, emotional, nonverbal, visual, artistic, holistic and spatial.

If you are more right-side oriented and your spouse is left-side oriented, how will you communicate? It's as though you speak different languages! And you probably do.

## The Brain

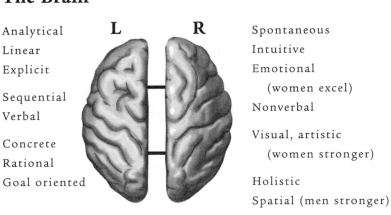

| | **L** | **R** | |
|---|---|---|---|
| Analytical | | | Spontaneous |
| Linear | | | Intuitive |
| Explicit | | | Emotional |
| | | | (women excel) |
| Sequential | | | Nonverbal |
| Verbal | | | |
| Concrete | | | Visual, artistic |
| Rational | | | (women stronger) |
| Goal oriented | | | Holistic |
| | | | Spatial (men stronger) |

Have you ever been in a class or even a church service where the speaker focused on dry, detailed facts? If he was inflexible, he was annoyed by interruptions to his train of thought, so after each distraction he would return to the beginning and review. The step-by-step speech was monotonous with little emotional expression. If so, you were listening to a person who was an extreme—and I mean extreme—left-brain dominant.

If you listen to a speaker or someone in a conversation who rambles from topic to topic, relies on his or her own opinions and feelings, is easily led away from the point, leaves gaps in the presentation to give the conclusion and uses emotional language and hunches, you're in the presence of the extreme right-brain dominant. The left side wants to know, "What's the bottom line?" The right side travels around the barn a few times to get there. And as you'll see later, personality differences will affect how a person responds.

When you were in school you probably ran into individuals who excelled in math or reading but flunked playground! Why? They were functioning with a highly advanced left brain, but the right brain was less developed.

A man who is a highly proficient chemist also enjoys social activities and goes  out dancing twice a week. Which portion of his brain is he using for these tasks? He is using the left side for his work, which must be careful, accurate and logical. When he's out dancing, he feels the steps by shifting to the right side of his brain. The chemist may be more comfortable using his left side, but he's able to make a switch for some right-brain activities. We shift back and forth between these two sides of the brain as we carry on our daily activities.

Remember, we will constantly reinforce our dominant side because it's easier to go that route than to break new ground by using the less dominant side.


## Brain Differences Between Men and Women

Let's go back in time and look at the brain differences in boys and girls. Let's assume you have X-ray glasses that allow you to look into their brains. As you look inside, you may see a discrepancy between boys and girls.

In the brain there is a section that connects the left and right hemispheres. It's a bundle of nerves (the technical name is *corpus callosum*) and there are up to 40 percent more of these nerve bundles in girls than in boys. This means that women are able to use both sides of the brain at the same time, whereas men have to switch from one side of the brain to the other, depending upon what they need. Women can enjoy more cross talk between both sides of the brain. In other words, women use their brains holistically.

This extra connective tissue in girls is a reason why they develop language skills earlier than boys and will use many more words than the young males of our species. Do you know why boys often read more poorly than girls? It's the brain again. *The brain that will read better is the brain that can use both sides of the brain at once.* Interestingly, it's also easier to "read" the emotions on a person's face when you use both sides of your brain simultaneously.

A woman's brain has been developed to express and verbalize. This is why throughout adulthood she wants to talk about it. A man's brain has been geared to develop his spatial skills. This is why throughout his life he wants to do something about it. That's why a woman is usually quicker to talk about her feelings, while a man wants to act quickly to do something about it.

Of course you recognize this is where the conflicts arise (and probably always will). A woman will say, "Let's sit down and talk this through." Meanwhile, the man is straining at the bit to get it fixed and get on with life! Remember, neither response is wrong and neither is better than the other.

In studies at the University of Pennsylvania, brain-scan equipment has been used to generate computer photographs of brains in use. They look almost like maps. The equipment produces pictures of the brain in different colors, with each color showing a different degree of intense cortical activity.

To get this mapping, a man and woman are hooked up to the equipment and both are asked to do a spatial task—to figure out how two objects fit together. If you were looking at a computer screen depicting the woman's brain, you would see that the color and intensity on both sides are fairly equal. But something else happens to the man's brain. The right side lights up with various colors that reflect a high degree of right-brain activity and much less activity in the left hemisphere. But if verbal skills are tested, watch out! The man uses much less of his brain compared with the woman's use of hers. Her left hemisphere really lights up!

Recently in a seminar, I had the opportunity to see such pictures. In a brain scan on a woman it showed activity on both sides of the brain when she was talking. When the man was talking, the brain scan indicated activity only on the left side of his brain.

The findings of this research indicate that a woman's brain is at work almost all the time in more sections than the man's. It's as if both hemispheres are always on call; whereas in a man's brain, one hemisphere at a time is on call.

Think of it like this: If there's a task to do, a man's brain turns on. When the task is completed, the brain turns off. But a woman's brain is always on. It's true that parts of a man's brain are always on, but when the two brains are compared in their downtime, or inactive time, the difference between the portion of the woman's brain that is always on and a man's that manifests an on/off function is quite pronounced.[2]

There are other results of the fact that women have 40 percent more, and thicker, nerve connectors between the two sides of the brain.

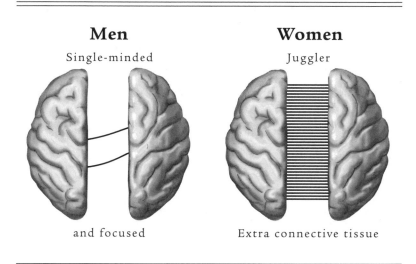

## Men

Single-minded

and focused

## Women

Juggler

Extra connective tissue

Women can tune in to everything going on around them. A wife may handle five hectic activities at one time while her husband is reading a magazine, totally oblivious to the various problems going on right under his nose. She can juggle more items but can be distracted more easily. He can focus on one task more effectively but can lose sight of other aspects. He has to stop one activity in order to attend to another.

The result of this difference causes women to be more perceptive than men about people. Women have a greater ability to pick up feelings and sense the difference between what people say and what they mean. Women's intuition has a physical basis. A woman's brain is like a computer that can integrate reason and intuition.

This drives some men crazy. There are numerous stories about couples who have gone out socially and the wife says to her husband, "I think there's a problem or something is going on." Her husband responds with, "How do you know? Where are the facts?" And she says, "I don't have any facts. I just sense it." He says, "You don't know what you're talking about." But a week later, when he finds out she was right, he's amazed and even more puzzled.

It could be that women pick up more information than men do since their sensitivities, such as hearing, eyesight, senses of taste and smell, are more heightened than men's.

The hearing difference is noted even in childhood. Men, in general, hear better in one ear. Females, in general, hear more data and hear equally well in both ears. All the way through life, males hear less than females say, which creates profound problems in relationships.

It has been noted that boys from very early on ignore voices, even parents' voices, more than girls do. Why? In some of these cases the boys are simply not hearing. They also do less well than girls at picking out background noises. Boys, quite simply, hear less background noise and differentiate less among various sounds. This is one of the reasons why parents and anyone around a boy often report having to speak louder to the boy than to a girl.[3]

What does this difference mean? It is the main reason why men are fixers—task oriented—and not as able to do several things at once. They need to focus on one thing at a time. When a man takes on a task at home, such as cleaning the garage or working in the yard, to him it's a single-focus task, *not a fellowship time*. If his wife wants to work with him, she usually wants to carry on a conversation at the same time. To him this may seem like an interruption—an invasion of his space, a distraction—and he reacts strongly to it. Millions and perhaps billions of conflicts over the years could have been avoided if men and women had not only understood this difference but honored it.

## When Differences Collide

Generally speaking, when it comes to approaching and solving problems, women use both sides of the brain and are able to create an overview. Men tend to break down the problem into pieces in order to come up with a solution. A man goes through steps 1, 2, 3 and 4 and has a solution. He uses a linear approach. A woman tends to go through steps 1, 3, 2 and 4 and reaches the same conclusion. If she arrives there before the man does, he probably won't accept her correct answer because he hasn't completed steps 1, 2, 3 and 4 yet. He's not ready for her answer.

A woman tends to feel that her husband isn't listening. He is, but he's not ready. A wife complains, "It's obvious; why can't you see it?" He can't see it because that's not the way he thinks.

A husband says, "Just take it one step at a time—you can't approach it that way." But she can. Neither the man's nor the woman's approach is wrong; they're just different. Can you imagine what a couple could accomplish if they learned to use each other's creativity and strength?[4]

Men like structure. Men like to put things in order. They like to regulate, organize, enumerate (men love to talk about numbers and statistics) and fit things into rules and patterns. It's not unusual for men to take the time to put their CDs and videos in alphabetical order or to figure out how long it takes to walk two miles or drive 85 miles to their favorite fishing hole.

Ever wonder why some men have a set routine on Saturdays? Maybe the order is wash the car, mow the lawn, trim the roses and take a nap. And it's always done at the same time in the same order.[5] Order provides structure and conserves energy. Keep the word "energy" in mind, for it's the source of contention between men and women.

The way in which men use their brains is an exclusive mode. (Some women refer to it as tunnel vision!) This mode can cause the man to exclude everything except what he is focusing on. It shuts out other possibilities. And men exert an abundance of energy to stay in this position. Most men like to know exactly where they are and what they are doing at a given point in time. It's a way to stay in control.

When a husband is at home and his attention is locked on the TV, on the newspaper or on fixing the car, he's in his exclusive mind-set. If his wife talks to him, he feels an interference or intrusion. *And for him it's an energy leak.* He hopes it will leave! When he does exert energy to shift from whatever he was doing to concentrate on his wife, he's upset because of the energy expenditure. He has to change his focus and shift it elsewhere because he can't handle both at once. She feels he's inconsiderate for not listening, and he feels she's inconsiderate because of the intrusion. Actually, neither is inconsiderate. They just don't understand the gender difference. If they did, they could each learn to respond differently.

Women are inclusive and can jump in and out of different topics. There's no energy drain for them. A woman actually picks up energy by entering into new experiences or changes. She is able to see the situation and beyond. She sees and responds to life like a camera with a wide-angle lens, whereas his camera has a highly focused microscope lens. He sees the tree in great detail; she sees the tree, but she also sees the grove and its potential. A woman's expectation of a man's perceptual ability should be tempered with this knowledge.[6]

Remember, there will be exceptions to what is said here. Some men and women will be just the opposite. My wife and I are exceptions. I tend to be the juggler and she is more single-minded. It also appears that personality preference (which is discussed in later chapters) has a modifying effect on some of these characteristics.

Here's another issue: Since a man focuses on one thing at a time and a woman can handle several things at one time, if she's doing multiple things while talking to him, he feels she's not paying attention to him. If she were interested, she would look at him with 100-percent attention. Does this scenario sound familiar?

> Men also can't understand how women can leave the the-ater or the living room during the most important part of a movie and go to the bathroom. A man will hold it! He has his priorities. He also has a larger bladder! On the other hand, the woman's "inclusive" mode gives her a sense of what's going on in the film, and she can still "watch" the film while she's in the bathroom. If the man is not physically watching the movie, he misses out. Even though she may not have caught all the details, she doesn't have a sense of missing anything.[7]

## Differences in Handling Feelings

This brings us to a question you've probably heard: Why can't men get into feelings like a woman does? The answer is that men have three strikes against them when it comes to feelings.

*One*, they're wired differently.

*Two*, they're raised to be emotionally handicapped. They're given neither the encouragement nor the training to learn to understand a wide range of feelings and to develop a vocabulary to express them. By the way, men and women do not have dif-ferent emotions. God created all of us as emotional beings. However, the way men and women deal with and express emo-tions may be different.

*Three*, the way women respond to men to find out their feel-ings often becomes counterproductive. Pressuring or even ask-ing a man "How do you feel?" usually doesn't work.

Again, we must look at the brain to see why men and women deal with their feelings in different ways.

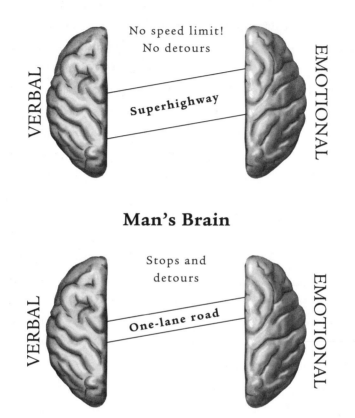

## Woman's Brain

VERBAL

No speed limit!
No detours

Superhighway

EMOTIONAL

## Man's Brain

VERBAL

Stops and
detours

One-lane road

EMOTIONAL

A woman has an immense number of neuroconnectors between her feelings and the "broadcasting studio" in her brain. She has an expressway that runs between her feelings and her speech. And because her brain is basically on all the time, it's very easy for her to share these feelings.

On the other hand, a man's brain has fewer nerve connectors between the right and left sides. No wonder he often has more of a struggle than a woman in expressing feelings. He doesn't have an expressway between feelings and the broadcasting area of the brain; it's more of a one-way road.[8]

That's why it's not easy for a man to share. If he attempts to put his feelings into words, he must take a prior step called *thought*. He has to ask, "I'm feeling something . . . what is it? All right, so that's what it is." Once he discovers his feelings, he must analyze them and decide what he can do about them.

A man's brain is a problem-solving brain. He is wired to have delayed reactions. When an emotional event occurs, he is not yet ready to express his feelings. He needs to move over to the left side of his brain and collect the words that will express his feelings. That's what stops many men from expressing emotions, they are somewhat vocabulary deficient.

It's not all their fault. Parents, teachers and society as a whole fail to provide much help in teaching men the vocabulary of feelings or the ability to paint word pictures to describe them. A man shares what he's able to share, and when new feelings arise, it's back to the drawing board to start the process all over again.

So remember this difference: *A man has to think about his feelings before he can share them. A woman can feel, talk and think at the same time.*[9]

A woman goes through a different sequence. When a woman is upset, what does she do first? She talks about it. And as she talks she is able to think about what she's saying and feeling. The end result is that she figures it out, usually by herself. She begins with feelings, then moves to talking and then to thinking.

Eventually she develops the ability to do all three at the same time:

Feeling————————*Talking* ————————Thinking

Because a woman problem-solves out loud, a man usually thinks he has caused the problem or that she wants him to solve the problem. It's possible that he could fix it, but only if she requests a solution. Almost every woman just wants her man to listen and reflect the fact that he has heard what she's saying.

A man is going to express his feelings in a different order. When feelings surface, most often he moves to taking action and then to thinking. When an upset occurs, his immediate response is to do something about it. That helps him to think it through. In time he learns to feel, act and think at the same time:

Feeling——————————— *Acting* ———————————Thinking

Notice that talking to resolve the problem isn't part of the formula for men. Communication is more significant for a woman; action is more significant for a man.[10] When a woman understands this, she doesn't have to be surprised by her man's reaction to emotion. She can accept his style and even encourage him to respond in this way as she adapts some of her typical responses to more nearly match his.

Keep in mind that each side of the brain has, as it were, its own language. If a man is stronger in his left brain (in other words, if he's left-brain dominant), his language is going to be concerned with facts and will tend to be logical and precise.

## What Do You Think?

1. To what extent does the previous description fit your spouse?
2. Based on what you have just read, how will this help you in responding to your spouse?

3. Do women talk more than men or do men talk more than women?

This whole business of relationships is about left-brained men and right-brained women being attracted to each other. If they are ever to communicate across their natural gender gap and if they are to develop into a functional couple, they must learn to understand and use the other person's language style to some extent. They must become bilingual! Can you make this switch?

## Learning Your Spouse's Language

The differences between the brains of men and women, which we have outlined, mean that when men and women communicate (or attempt to!) they have different purposes in mind. Women speak and hear a language of connection and intimacy, whereas a man tends to speak and hear a language of status and independence.

Men speak *report*-talk. They like to express knowledge and skills. They use talking as a way to get and keep attention.

Women speak *rapport*-talk. It's their way of establishing connection and negotiating relationships.[11]

So what you have is not really a difference of dialects within the same language but cross-cultural communication. It's been said that men and women speak different "genderlects."[12]

This area of difference is not just a concern in marriage but in the workplace as well:

The male-female difference represents the biggest culture gap that exists. If you can learn the skills and attitudes to bridge the gender differences in communication, you will have mastered what it takes to communicate and negotiate with almost anyone about almost anything.[13]

A new word, "genderflex," has been coined for this situation. It's not in the dictionary yet, but it will be. The word means to temporarily use communication patterns typical of the other gender in order to connect with them and increase the potential for influence.[14]

This is an adaptive approach to communication, designed to improve relationships and performance. It's doesn't mean a change in personality, lifestyle or values. It's an adaption that will actually create greater flexibility and growth among those who practice it. It requires choosing to adopt the style, content and structure of the other gender's communication patterns. You are not becoming like the other gender, but you are showing that you understand how he or she communicates.

## Women Express, Men Resolve

Those who use genderflex talk will remember that women tend to speak the language of expressers and men the language of resolvers. For example, women typically are expanders in the content of what they share, while most men are condensers. That is, women tend to give much more detail and include feelings, whereas men tend to give bottom-line, factual information. When speaking a man's language, a woman—even if she were talking about interpersonal situations—would use more factual descriptions that focus on identifying a problem or a solution rather than use an abundance of details or feelings. And a man would give not only bottom-line facts but descriptive details with an emphasis on the interpersonal.[15]

Keep in mind that you will find exceptions to these male-female styles of communication. Some men will express themselves as expanders, and some women will express themselves as condensers. This is probably due to the influence of personality variation.

By the way, are you aware that men talk more than women? It's true! There hasn't been a single study that gives any evidence that women talk more than men, but there are numerous studies showing that men talk more than women.[16] However, women do talk much more than men on subjects of people, feelings and relationships, just as men talk more than women on their preferred subjects.

Many men will say they prefer talking to women rather than men because women are better at conversation. What women actually are better at is listening. They are skilled at the art of supporting other people's conversational efforts, encouraging them to go on, enabling them to explain fully, and reinforcing their conversational efforts with smiles, head nods, good eye contact and other indications of attentiveness.

Women have been raised to use communication as a mechanism for creating relationship bonds. Men have been encouraged to communicate primarily to exchange information.

Certain words and categories of words appear much more frequently in women's speech than in men's. Adverbs of intensity, such as "awfully," "terribly," "pretty," "quite," "so," and the adjectives "charming," "lovely," "adorable," "divine," "cute" and "sweet" are more common in women's usage.

Women also have a much more extensive vocabulary for colors. Words like "taupe," "beige," "mauve," "lavender" and "violet" are not common in men's speech. Males are not expected to discuss the lovely mauve drapes in the conference room, or the streaks of lavender in the sunset.

## Creating Bonds and Exchanging Information

Men and women have been taught to use language differently. For women, speech communication is basically for social relationships. Women have been raised to use communication as a mechanism for creating bonds. Men have been encouraged to communicate primarily to exchange information.

Most men tend to feel more comfortable speaking in public than in private, intimate conversations. The opposite is true for most women. They enjoy one-on-one conversations because they are more personal and intimate and they build relationships. For most men, conversation is used to gain status, to negotiate, to solve problems, to get attention and even to keep their independence.[17]

# Getting the Response You Desire

Communicating for change involves making requests. But too often requests sound like demands. Timing is essential when a husband or wife makes a request. If a husband asks for something when his wife is in the midst of some project, he can't expect an immediate response. And perhaps he doesn't, but his wife may interpret that he wants an immediate response. It might be good for a man to say, "I'm not asking for it or needing it right now, I just want to know if . . ." or "Could you get this by tomorrow?"

If a wife sees her husband just about to do a task, it's best not to ask him to do what he obviously is going to do. And if he's focused on some project, she can wait or leave him a note for the next task.

Author John Gray presented an interesting concept by making a very precise suggestion for women when they ask their husbands to do something. When asking a man to do a task, it's important to ask, "Would you?" rather than, "Could you?" When the word "could" is used, it's like asking him if he's able. The phrase "Would you?" asks for a decision as well as a commitment.

Here are some examples of indirect and direct requests:

| Indirect Request | Direct Request |
| --- | --- |
| The kids need to be picked up and I can't do it. | Would you pick up the kids? |
| The groceries are in the car. | Would you bring in the groceries? |
| I can't fit anything else in the trash can. | Would you empty the trash? |
| The backyard is really a mess. | Would you clean up the backyard? |
| We haven't gone out in weeks. | Would you take me out this week?[18] |

There are also some words that strike fear into a man's heart. Those words are:

"Let's talk" or "I need to talk to you"

A man will interpret those words as:

Code blue
Man overboard
I'm going to get dumped on

To a woman, those same words can mean:

Let's get together
Come closer
Let's problem solve together
I have so much to tell you

Usually a woman says, "Let's talk" or "We need to talk," when something is wrong. It's no wonder men tend to be gun-shy when they hear those words. It may help if a wife would say, "Let's talk," when she wants to praise her husband![19]

Both men and women think, *Why should I go to all this work of adapting and changing? If my partner would talk less (or talk more) and listen, everything would be all right.* Here's the true question to ask: *Is what I am doing working? If not, why keep doing it?* There is a better way.

## What's Your Plan?

1. In light of this information on gender language, how will you respond differently to your spouse?
2. How would you like your spouse to respond to you?

*Notes*

1. Michael McGill, *The McGill Report on Male Intimacy* (San Francisco: Harper & Row, 1985), p. 74.

2. Michael Gurian, *The Wonder of Boys* (New York: G. P. Putnam, 1996), pp. 11-15, adapted.

3. Ibid., pp. 16, 17, adapted.

4. Joe Tanenbaum, *Male and Female Realities* (San Marcos, Calif.: Robert Erdmann Publishing, 1990), pp. 96, 97, adapted.

5. Joan Shapiro, *Men, A Translation for Women* (New York: Avon Books, 1992), pp. 71-84, adapted.

6. Tanenbaum, *Male and Female Realities*, pp. 40, 82, adapted; Jacquelyn Wonder and Pricilla Donovan, *Whole Brain Thinking* (New York: William Morrow & Company, 1984), pp. 18-34, adapted.

7. Tanenbaum, *Male and Female Realities*, p. 90.

8. Gurian, *The Wonder of Boys*, p. 23, adapted.

9. John Gray, *What Your Mother Couldn't Tell You and Your Father Didn't Know* (New York: HarperCollins, 1994), p. 90; Tanenbaum, *Male and Female Realities*, chaps. 4-6. See also John Gray, *Mars and Venus Together Forever,* and his even more popular *Men Are from Mars and Women Are from Venus,* both from HarperCollins.

10. Gray, *What Your Mother Couldn't Tell You and Your Father Didn't Know*, pp. 90, 91, adapted.

11. Deborah Tannen, *You Just Don't Understand* (New York: Morrow Publishing, 1990), pp. 42, 77, adapted.

12. Judith C. Tingley, *Genderflex* (New York: Amacom, 1993), p. 16, adapted.

13. *Transcultural Leadership, Empowering the Diverse Work Force* (Houston, Tex.: Gulf Publishing, 1993), n.p.

14. Tingley, *Genderflex*, p. 16.

15. Ibid., p. 19, adapted.

16. Ibid., p. 29, adapted.

17. Tannen, *You Just Don't Understand,* p. 77, adapted.

18. Gray, *What Your Mother Couldn't Tell You and Your Father Didn't Know*, p. 250.

19. Sharyn Wolf, *How to Stay Lovers for Life* (New York: Dutton, 1997), pp. 38, 39.

# WHAT ABOUT PERSONALITY?
### CHAPTER EIGHT

Have you ever been frustrated with your spouse because he or she always seems preoccupied with heaven-only-knows what?

Do you start the day with great intentions to get a few specific things done but get distracted?

Have you ever been excited about going to a church fellowship so that you can spend time with a lot of your friends, but your partner complains about having to endure another evening of shallow conversation?

Does it ever surprise you that people view you as insensitive and uncaring, when deep down inside you are very sensitive and care deeply for others?

Have you ever left a social gathering confident that you've made a good impression, only to find as you drive home with your spouse that there were at least 10 things you could have said better or shouldn't have said at all?

Do you have friends who seem to be calm and relaxed, with ample time to play, while you feel like a hamster on a treadmill?

# Different Folks, Different Strokes

Nowhere is the breadth of God's creativity more evident than in humankind. No two of us are exactly alike. Even identical twins can have opposite personalities. Each of us has a combination of gifts, talents, attitudes, beliefs, needs and wants that is different from anyone else's. That's part of what makes life so exciting. It's all right to be different! But is it all right for your partner to be different?

If you have ever observed families with more than one child, you've probably been amazed that children from the same gene pool, raised by the same parents, in the same neighborhood, eating the same diet, going to the same school and church, can be totally different. What accounts for these differences?

Why do some people love to be alone for hours on end and others go crazy if people aren't around? Why does one person always comes up with new ideas and invent things while another is content to use things the way they're "supposed" to be used? Why do some people like to talk things out while others prefer to work it out for themselves and then talk about it? Why does one person welcome a new employee and another act as if it's the end of the world? How can some people read a book for an hour without being bored or distracted, while others start climbing the wall after only ten minutes? Why do some people take pride in having a clean and neat office while other offices appear as if they've been used for nuclear testing?

In Psalm 139:14 (*TLB*) we read, "Thank you for making me so wonderfully complex! It is amazing to think about. Your workmanship is marvelous—and how well I know it." The Bible clearly teaches that every person is made in the image of God and is of infinite worth and value.

As we've looked at some of the differences between men and women and their communication styles, you may have been thinking, *But not all men are alike! Some men are so different from other men. Some women are so . . . Why is that? When I meet someone new, how do I figure out the best way to talk to him or her?*

Differences in personality types are the reason you see such variations among people.

## Understanding Personality Type

What is personality type? How does it work? Personality type consists of several inborn preferences or tendencies that have a strong impact on how we develop as individuals. Each of us begins life with a small number of inherited personality traits that make us a little different from everyone else. Do you know what some of your traits are? What was it about you that made you a little bit (or a lot) different from your mom and dad, brother or sister?

Personality type consists of several inborn preferences or tendencies that have a strong impact on how we develop as individuals.

Each trait is a fundamental building block of personality. These basic inborn traits determine many individual differences in personality. While core traits are present at birth, they are influenced and modified by our environment and how we are reared.

There are numerous personality theories and explanations. The one we are going to use is the *Myers-Briggs Type Indicator* (MBTI). It provides a practical way to identify, translate, and understand core differences in personality. The MBTI identifies four sets of contrasting personality traits or *preferences*: extroversion and introversion, sensing and intuition, thinking and feeling, judging and perceiving. Each trait can be identified by its complete name or by the single letter assigned to it. A preference is the conscious or unconscious choice a person makes in a certain designated realm.

How People Gather Energy and Respond
Extroversion (E)_____(I) Introversion

How People Gather Data and Information
Sensing (S)_____(N) Intuition

How People Make Decisions—by Their Heads or Hearts
Thinking (T)_____(F) Feeling

How People Structure Their Lives
Judging (J)_____(P) Perceiving

According to type theory, everyone uses all eight of the traits, but one trait out of each pair is preferred and more fully developed. This is similar to the fact that while we have two hands and use both of them, we tend to prefer using one hand over the other. Most people are either right-handed or left-handed. When using your preferred hand, tasks are usually easier, take less time, are less frustrating, and the end result is usually better.

As I present the various preferences, you will notice many variations. For example, one extrovert may fit all of the characteristics mentioned. In fact, on a scale of 0 to 10, this particular E may be a 10 and would be what we call a Total E, whereas another extrovert may be a 6 on the scale. Some people may find themselves having characteristics of both preferences in each pair. It's quite normal if a person does not have a strong preference either way.

This MBTI is a tool that doesn't stereotype people or place them in watertight boxes. It's more like a zip code. It tells you the state, city and neighborhood but not the specific address.

A key aspect of the MBTI is its nonjudgmental nature. The MBTI was grounded in the belief that while different approaches to interacting exist among individuals, no one set of preferences is better or worse than any alternative set of preferences. Thus, the MBTI does not attempt to change behavior to meet a given ideal; rather it encourages individuals to understand and appreciate their own and others' personality preferences.

It is possible to be extreme and never access a nonpreferred trait. Then your strength maximized becomes your liability. As with drinking, eating or certain other things, too much of a good thing can lead to trouble. If you have any one preference too strongly or too clearly defined, it may be a curse rather than a blessing.

## What Do You Think?

1. What are your thoughts about the value of a personality type?
2. What are five descriptive adjectives you would use to describe yourself?

3. What are five descriptive adjectives you would use to
   describe your spouse?

We will discuss some personality types after Jim and Alice
talk about their differences and how they've learned to adjust to
them. Here is Jim's story:

My name is Jim. I'd like to tell you about my outgoing,
social wife. That's what I call her now, and that's what I
called her before we married. But after about two years of
marriage I started calling her "Mouth"! She talked and
talked. She even talked to herself. Now me, I'm just the
opposite. I don't talk much at all. At first I was attracted to
her talk. Then I was repulsed by it. My ears got exhausted.

I couldn't understand why Alice had to think out
loud so much. It's like she wanted the whole world to
know about her wild ideas. And it's not just because
she's a woman. I've seen men who are the same way. But
it seemed like she would start talking before she engaged
her brain. At times I felt like my space was being invaded
by her running commentary on everything or by saying
the same things over and over or wanting an immediate
response from me on a question I'd never had a chance
to think about. Man, all that stuff wore me out.

There were even times when I'd go to the garage to
putter around (and find some peace and quiet) and Alice
would come out there and bring up a subject, ask my
opinion and arrive at her own conclusion before I could
even think about it. I'd just stand there shaking my head
and wonder, *Why even ask me?*

When we go to an activity, it's like she knows everyone there and wants to stay forever. It's like she could

never run down or get enough socializing. I've seen men like that, too. I've always wondered how they did it. It drains me, but it seems to give her a shot of adrenaline!

Oh, and then wait until you hear this: I think I'm a caring guy. I do give compliments. Maybe not as many as I could, but I don't think I could ever give enough to Alice. She is so capable and gifted. But it seems like she doesn't believe it unless I or someone else tells her. I used to wonder why she would ask me how she did or how she looked when the answer was obvious. Fantastic!

And something else that really bugged me—Alice is better about this now—she would interrupt me when we talked. It takes me longer to get things out and to reach a conclusion. So, if I talked or thought too slowly, I either got interrupted or she finished my statement for me. We had a good discussion (argument) over that one. But she's much better now, and I don't avoid discussions with her. Sometimes I remind her that our speed of thinking and speaking are different, and that helps.

When we have a conflict, I think (or used to think) there is just too much talking about the problem. Alice had the belief that if we just talked it through a bit more, everything would get resolved! Resolved? A few more words would be the last straw. We eventually learned to put some time limits on each segment of the conversation so I could have time to think. Then I was ready to continue on. I also worked on sharing my first reaction without having to do so much thinking and editing.

Now and then I've said to Alice, "Honey, I want you to resolve this; but for me to continue, since I'm getting worn down, why don't you write out what you're thinking or put your thoughts on the computer. Then I can read them over and be able to respond. OK?" That has worked well for us, and that way Alice doesn't get as loud either, since I really tend to withdraw from that. I used to tell her, "You're not going to get me to respond by shouting at me. It won't work." Now I say, "I want to hear you. I would appreciate it if you would say it softly and give me a chance to respond."

Sometimes I would ask her, "Why are you bringing that up again? We've already talked about it." Alice would say, "No, we haven't." And then we would argue over whether we had or not. This went on for years, until one day I heard her say, "Could it be that you rehearse conversations in your mind and then think we've already talked about it?" Bingo! That's exactly what I do, and when she said it, I realized it. Fortunately, we've learned to laugh about it. Sometimes I catch myself and say, "Yeah, I did talk to you about it . . . in my head."

Sometimes I worry about what Alice says to others about us and our intimacy. You know, our lovemaking. She likes to talk about it when we're not even doing it, and sometimes during a romantic time she wants to talk. That's not me. I don't say much, but I've learned this is what Alice enjoys. And it's getting more comfortable.

What has really helped me (and us) is to realize there's nothing wrong with Alice the way she is. That's just her. It's the way she's wired. I guess it's the way God created her. She's OK; I'm OK. We're just different, and we can learn to adjust.

I've learned to appreciate the fact that she's helped me to be more social and involved with other people. It's apparent that Alice needs more interaction and time with people than I do. Now I'm glad to provide it. It's all right for her to go places and gab, and I can stay home or get together with one of my male friends.

It has really helped me to understand that Alice needs to talk out loud to figure things out. And it doesn't mean she's going to do what she's thinking out loud. She's just thinking. I've learned not to assume.

We're not perfect, but we're much more accepting. We've learned to be creative in the ways we approach each other. And it's a lot more peaceful.

Alice shares the story of her journey:

Well, I'll try to be brief (that's a joke!). I'm an outgoing, talkative person who, for some strange reason, was drawn to a quiet, reserved, thoughtful man. I knew we were different when we were dating but never realized just how much until we were married. When it really hit me was the evening I figured out that Jim seemed to be avoiding me. Even when I was talking to him it seemed like he couldn't wait until I quit talking. And his responses got shorter and shorter. It was as though he thought that if he said less, I wouldn't have so much to respond to. I guess it was true, because eventually I'd get fed up and socialize on the phone. I actually felt rejected and hurt because I wasn't getting enough talk out of Jim. I couldn't figure out why he was like that. At first I thought, *That's just the way men are.* But others I had dated weren't always like that. In fact, I've known women who are like Jim. So I figured it's just the way he's wired and put together.

I just love getting together with other people. I get energized by them. But it doesn't take long (at least it seems to me) for Jim to get worn out at a party and want to leave early. I've even seen him just sit off to one side by himself or go into another room for a while just to be alone. I used to think, *What's wrong with that man?* Then I began to discover that Jim needs some quiet time and space to get energy back. That's draining for me, but it perks him up.

He's friendly and communicates well, but he doesn't go out of his way to connect with people. I've got scads of friends. He's satisfied with just two. See, there's the difference—just two! That wouldn't be enough for me. I need more people to talk with. And I love interruptions. They're just great, but they really bother Jim. It's like he needs to know ahead of time that he's going to be interrupted.

One of our biggest conflicts is, or was, in the area of communication. I like to get things resolved, and that means talking through every part of an issue. But when we talked, or when I talked, the more I talked the more he seemed to retreat. So I figured I should just keep after him and he would be bound to open up. No such luck! He'd retreat, clam up, or say, "I don't know." I admit I want answers right now. I used to say, "Jim, tell me right now. You don't need time. For Pete's sake, tell me!" And then nothing. Silence. It's like I short-circuited his thinking ability. And later on I discovered I had!

Jim is more of what they call an inner person. Through some reading I discovered he's the kind of person who likes to think things through in the quiet privacy of his mind, without pressure—and then he's got a lot to say! Little did I know this. Now when I need his feedback or a discussion, I just go to him and say, "Jim, here's something I'd like you to think about. Put it on the back burner where it can simmer for a while. When it's done, let's discuss it." He appreciates it and we talk more. And lest you think he always uses a crockpot to cook, he doesn't. Sometimes it's a microwave! After I did this for a while, he said to me, "Thanks for recognizing and respecting my need to think things through in the privacy of my mind." That felt good, because I like compliments.

I've had to learn that he isn't comfortable thinking and talking fast out loud. That's my world, not his. A few times we got into conflicts in which I pressured him so much that he just let fly with outbursts that seemed extreme. I learned not to push. It's better to let him think first.

I've also learned not to interrupt Jim with every thought that pops into my head. I'm finally learning to edit my thoughts and pick times when I can have his attention. I know my thinking out loud used to bother him because he thought I meant every word of it. I just like to sort things out and I don't care who knows it. So now I just warn him by saying, "Jim, I'm just thinking out loud again. You can relax, because I'm not going to rearrange all the furniture in the house today."

You know, I used to think that Jim's quietness and withdrawal at times was a passive-aggressive way of getting back at me. But it wasn't. God made me unique and made Jim the way he is. I just didn't understand it. Twice this last month he actually did some thinking out loud with me, which was wonderful. I know it was difficult for Jim, but it was great to see him put forth that effort.

I hate to admit it, I really do, but I see some value in being alone and quiet . . . sometimes . . . just a bit.

I've also learned that when I encourage him to be who he is, I receive more of what I need. The other day, I knew he was frazzled, but I wanted to talk. Usually, I would have forced the discussion or tried to, but I remembered a couple of passages from Proverbs: "Don't talk so much. You keep putting your foot in your mouth. Be sensible and turn off the flow!" (Prov. 10:19, *TLB*). "Self-control means controlling the tongue! A quick retort can ruin everything" (Prov. 13:3, *TLB*).

So I said to Jim, "You look like you need some time to recoup. Why don't you go read or do whatever, and maybe we could talk a bit later." And we did talk—quite a bit. And I am learning to write him notes, too.

Jim understands things that used to really get me. He's better at it, but I've learned that a few of his words mean a hundred of mine. When he gets a big smile on his face and doesn't say much, I say, "It looks like that smile is about 500 of my words." And he says, "You've got that right. I just love good translators!"

So I've learned to give him time and space and not to interrupt when he talks. And I don't assume anymore that he doesn't have opinions or want to talk. He's selective and more methodical, whereas I use a scatter-gun approach.

Well, there they are—Jim and Alice. Each married to an opposite. And you know what? Neither person's style is wrong. Each was created in a unique way. Did you identify with one of them? Or perhaps you saw a bit of both in you.

## What Do You Think?

1. With whom did you identify the most, Jim or Alice?
2. List five of the characteristics mentioned that also identify you.
3. What suggestions would you make to enable an E and an I to communicate in a more effective way?

Let's summarize what an E and an I are like. You have your own definitions of what an extrovert and an introvert are, but let's be clear about them. These qualities delineate the way people prefer to interact with the environment or the way they are energized.

## Extroversion

Remember, an extrovert (E) gains energy from people. E's are people oriented. An introvert (I) is energized by being alone and is privacy oriented.

The extroversion (E) and introversion (I) preferences focus on how we gain energy. We are like batteries. When a battery is attached to a charger, energy flows into the battery. When the battery is powering a lightbulb, energy flows out of the battery.

Energy flows *into* extroverted types when they are around people. Energy flows *out* of extroverted types when they are quietly reflecting on issues. In contrast, energy flows *into* introverted types when they are able to reflect quietly, while energy flows *out* of them when they are interacting with others.

An E is a social creature. People energy is what they feed on. They are approachable by friends and strangers alike. Sometimes they may tend to dominate a conversation. Invite them to a six-hour party and they're on cloud nine. At the end of the party

Energy

flows into

extroverted

types when

they are

around

people;

energy flows

into

introverted

types when

they are able

to reflect

quietly.

they're wired and ready to go out with friends for coffee at Denny's. They talk with everyone; in fact, they may share too much too soon on a personal level, which may concern an introvert partner.

E's are not the best listeners. For them, listening is harder than talking because they have to give up the limelight. They may also have a tendency to interrupt.

E's have been described as walking mouths. Instead of thinking first, they talk first and really have no idea what they're going to say until they hear themselves talking. They brainstorm out loud for the entire world to hear and often need to think out loud to come up with the answer. The ideas they come up with aren't set in concrete. They're still working them out, but they let everyone else in on the process. They tend to talk faster and louder and are a bit more animated. E's also prefer a large playing field in life without too many boundaries.

E's typically like noise. They look forward to the interruption of phone calls, and if the phone doesn't ring, they'll start calling people. When they come home, they turn on the TV and/or stereo, even though they don't watch or listen. They like background noise.

In conflict they talk louder and faster and believe that if they can say just one more thing, everything will be fine.

E's get lonely when their partner isn't there. They look forward to doing things with their partner rather than just sitting around. Judging from the way E's connect with people, you would think they are very secure; but E's have a high need for affirmation and compliments from everyone, especially from significant people. E's may think they've done a good job, but they won't believe it until they hear it from someone else. They may ask for an opinion, too. In other words, they *need*.

## Introversion

I's, on the other hand, need to formulate in the privacy of their thoughts what they are going to say before they are ready to share. If pressured to give an immediate, quick answer, their minds shut down. They usually respond with, "Let me think about that" or "I'll get back to you on that."

Often they are seen as shy or reserved. They prefer to share their time with one other person or a few close friends. They are usually quiet among strangers. They love privacy and quiet time to themselves. They learn how to concentrate and shut out noise.

Invite an I to a six-hour party and she would respond, "Six hours! You've got to be kidding. What will I do for six hours? I'd be wiped out!" So the introvert goes late, talks to selected people one at a time and leaves early. That is what's comfortable to them. They may not care for the fellowship time in a Sunday School class or church service, either.

I's are good listeners and hate to be interrupted when they talk. When they're in a relationship they tend to keep their thoughts to themselves and wish their partner would, too, if he or she is an E. I's also tend to be cautious when entering a new relationship.

When asked a question, I's usually take an average of seven seconds before responding. (The problem is, if the other person is an E, that person usually waits about a second and a half before jumping in to give an answer.) Our schools are geared to E children. When the teacher asks a question, all the E children raise their hands, even though they don't know the answer yet. They will formulate the answer as they talk out loud. It would level the playing field if the teacher would say to the class, "Here's a question for you. I'd like all of you to think about your answer for 20 seconds, and then I'll tell you when to raise your hands." A statement like that gives equal opportunity to the I's, who wish other people would rehearse their thoughts before speaking.

As you learned while reading about Jim, I's carry on great conversations with themselves, including what the other person said and their own responses. They can do this so realistically that they believe the conversation actually occurred.

I's are suspicious of compliments. In turn they may give them out sparingly. So if the partner of an I is an E, how might this affect the relationship?

When I's are married, they can handle the other person's absence fairly well. Usually they prefer just being with the other person, without a lot of activity and noise, and are more comfortable with a smaller playing field—one they can control. They have clearly defined boundaries and their motto is "You stay out of my territory and I'll stay out of yours."

## E and I Compatibility

Can an E and an I be compatible . . . and what if we're talking about an extreme I or E? You may assume that two E's and two I's would be more compatible because of their similarities. But other aspects of our personalities need to be factored in because they play a part in the compatibility equation. Frankly, any two personality combinations take work to become compatible.

An E and an I couple may experience more excitement and romance in their relationship. The downside is they may have to work harder at being compatible. Couples who have the same preference or who are closer together in preference may find that compatibility comes more easily, but they need to work on bringing stimulating ideas and resources into their relationship or risk getting into a rut!

The very factor that attracted the E and I to each other before marriage can be the major issue of conflict after marriage, as each person's preference will seem more extreme when viewed in daily proximity.

What can two different preference types do to be compatible? They can accept and verbally praise their partner's differences and uniqueness and avoid trying to make the other into a revised edition of their own preferences.

They can praise God for the strengths in each preference, such as the E's ability to connect socially and the I's stability, strength and depth of thinking.

E's need to remember that I's can be exhausted by superficial socializing. Introverts prefer less-frequent get-togethers with just a few people, particularly with those they feel comfortable being around. An E can help in a large social gathering by *not* introducing his or her I partner to everyone (which makes the I the center of attention an interminable number of times), by not talking too loudly, by not revealing personal items about their relationship and by not calling on them to pray out loud or asking them a question that requires an immediate response.

When an E wants to talk to an I, it's helpful to approach the I this way: "Here's something I'm interested in knowing. Why don't you think about it and let me know your response." An introvert will love this. An extrovert could also single out individuals with whom his I partner would be comfortable in one-on-one conversations.

An E may want to ask her I partner to let her know when his battery has been drained and he needs to leave. But I's also need to remember that an E partner thrives on being with people. One solution would be for an I to encourage his or her partner to go to the party before they do in order to have more time to socialize. Above all, an I needs to give an E partner more compliments than the I thinks is necessary.

One woman married into a family of eight (that's right, *eight!*) extreme extroverts. At family get-togethers she can only last for about an hour. Then she takes a half-hour break alone in another room to revitalize. You might think that's ridiculous or rude. No, it's reality—and the only way it can work. The other family members now understand the difference and accept it.

We can't fight the way God created us as unique beings. But we must seek balance as well as meet one another's needs.

When I's hear their E partners brainstorming out loud, they shouldn't assume that what they hear is fact. The E is just processing aloud for the whole world to hear. Just ask the E, "Are you brainstorming again?" and you'll probably hear a yes. On the other hand, it would be helpful for E's to announce they are doing this when it occurs. And when an I is thinking about something, it would be helpful to let the E know instead of letting the E feel ignored. It's easy for an E to feel rejected when the I doesn't say anything (even though there's a lot of talking going on inside the I's mind).

Let's look at another marriage scenario. Suppose the husband is as much of an E as an E can be, and his wife is an I. She doesn't say much in a group, but with close friends she talks more than her husband. He would love to have the house filled with people every Sunday afternoon. For her, three or four times a year is sufficient. How do they work this out? They have three couples over once a month after church. The wife knows two of the couples and feels comfortable with them. The other couple is new to her, but in a small group she can get to know them. This E and I have learned to be compatible.

What about you? What could you do to blend and grow your relationship? Remember, you can grow from these differences.[1]

## What's Your Plan?

1. Go back through the chapter and write down each characteristic that describes you. (You may find some description that fits on both sides of the fence.)
2. List how you will respond differently and how you would like your spouse to respond differently in order to become more compatible.
3. Which characteristic about your spouse has been the most difficult for you to understand?

*Note*

1. Sandra Hirsh and Jean Kummerow, *Life Types* (New York: Warner Books, 1989), p. 16, adapted; Otto Kroeger and Janet M. Thuesen, *Type Talk* (New York: Bantam Books, 1988), pp. 15, 16, adapted; David Luecke, *Prescription for Marriage* (Columbia, Md.: The Relationship Institute, 1989), pp. 54, 55, adapted.

# DIFFERENT WAYS TO GATHER INFORMATION

—————— CHAPTER NINE ——————

The next set of preferences has a profound impact on communication and intimacy in your marital relationship. These preferences reflect what sort of information you gather, how you gather it, the way you pay attention to the information you gather and the way you share it. You are either what we call a sensor (S) or an intuitive (N).

## How a Sensor Processes Information

If you're a sensor (S), you are keyed into information you receive through your five senses. What you pay attention to are the facts and details of situations. This is what you perceive or notice. It's what you believe.

What is it like to be a sensor? It really shows up in communication. When you ask a question, you want a specific answer (and that's the way you give answers). If you ask your spouse, "What time should I meet you?" and she says, "Around 4:00," that just won't do. You may ask, "Does that mean 3:55, 4:00 or 4:05?" You're that literal. I used to go fishing with a friend who was extreme in this regard. Anyone knows that when you ask your fishing partner if he has the bait over there, you're asking him to pass it to you. But when I'd ask Phil if he had the bait over there, he'd say, "Yes," and that was it. He wouldn't pass the bait until I said, "Will you please pass the bait?"

If someone asks you if you have the time, you say, "Yes," but you don't tell the person the time until they ask. You don't assume; you force others to be specific.

If you're looking at something and thinking of purchasing it and your partner says, "It's a good deal; it's less that $100," that won't do either. You want the bottom line. (Remember, the stronger your preference in this area, the more you are like this.)

As an S, you tend to be a focused person. You have a high level of concentration on what you're doing at the present. The future? You'll deal with it when it arrives. You don't waste time wondering what's next.

As a S, you are a doer. If you have a choice between sitting around thinking about something and performing a task, there's no question as to what you'll do. And you want to invest your efforts in tasks that yield results you can see.

You're a factual person. Theories don't thrill you, but good old facts do. This probably affects the type and style of preaching or teaching you respond to. When you hear something from another person, you want it presented sequentially—A to B to C to D. You don't like it when others meander off the path.

S's have little use for fantasy. They wonder why people assume, speculate and imagine. What good does it do?

One of the biggest frustrations for S's is when others don't give them clear guidelines or instructions. After all, they are very explicit and detailed. So it really bothers them when they receive instructions that are just general guidelines. If you ask an intuitive (N), "Where's the nearest Starbucks coffee store?" he will say, "Go to 17th Street and turn left. It's a couple of blocks down on the right. You can't miss it." But a sensor would say, "Turn around and go back out the way you came in. Turn left and go a block and a half to 17th Street and turn left. It's three-and-a-half blocks down on the left sandwiched between Kentucky Fried Chicken and a dry cleaners in a brick building."

S's have difficulty seeing the overall plan of something because they focus on what they're doing; they see the individual tree but not the forest.

When it comes to money (which can be a source of major conflict in a relationship), S's are very exacting. Money to them is tangible. When they have it, they can use it but only as much as the amount allows.[1] The S's view of money is that it's a tool to be used. That's it. In a relationship, an S probably looks at money realistically, rather than through rose-colored glasses.

Predictability in a relationship gives them a sense of security, whereas change throws them.

## N's and the Intuitive World

If your preference is intuitive (N), the way you respond to the world is *not* through the five senses or by means of facts, but on the basis of your sixth sense, or on hunches. Details and facts have their place (perhaps), but you can easily become bored with them. You don't take things at face value; instead, you look for the underlying meaning of relationships. You look for *possibilities*. "Possibility" is a very important word to an N, whose focus is not on the here and now but on the future.

If you are a sensor, you pay attention to facts and details and are more comfortable with *what* exists. If you are an intuitive, you look for the underlying meaning of relationships and prefer to look for *possibilities*.

N's are sometimes perceived as a bit absentminded. Why? Simply because they like to think of several things at once. Sometimes it's difficult to concentrate on what's going on at the moment because the future has so many intriguing possibilities. Intuitives live for the future. Today? Its purpose is to help get ready for tomorrow! If an N is going on a trip somewhere, it already started weeks in advance for this type who experiences it all during the preparation time. But for the S, the trip doesn't begin until arriving at the destination. Then an S can begin to experience it.

There is another significant difference between an S and an N. When the N is describing something, it's as though he's actually experiencing what he's describing. One couple I know had different preferences. Jim was an intuitive and Shelia a sensor. He had traveled a great deal during college, but Shelia had never left Nebraska until she married.

They had been married a little over a year when Jim told her of the dream vacation he wanted them to take the next summer. He wanted to explore Canada and Alaska. He told her of the possibility (there's that word again) of getting another couple to go with them and described what it would be like to drive from San Diego all the way to Vancouver, B.C., and then continue on to Anchorage, Alaska. It wouldn't cost that much since they could take tents and sleeping bags and stay in campgrounds all the way. He told her of the places and signs and wildlife they would see and experience. The more he talked, the more expressive and involved he became. It was almost real to him in its description.

By the time Jim finished, he was expecting Shelia to be just as enthusiastic as he was. It didn't happen. She was anything but thrilled with the idea, since her practical preference saw all sorts of problems. The questions rolled out one after the other. "How can we afford to take the time?" "What if the car breaks down?" "Is it really safe to camp?" "Where will we eat?" "What about showers?"

Jim felt crushed. He had thought Shelia would respond the way he felt. He had shared a dream with her. He hadn't said it was a dream; he had presented it as though it would happen. Shelia had taken everything he said literally and felt overwhelmed. If Jim had presented the trip in her language—in a factual manner—and had anticipated her questions and given detailed answers, she would have responded more favorably. Jim had been communicating as if he were talking to another intuitive.

N's have a unique way of dealing with time—to them it's relative. They may have a watch, but it doesn't help them to be on time. "Late" doesn't register unless an event has started without them. They may also be late because they tried to do too much; they thought they could complete those five tasks before they had to leave for the meeting. By the time they were supposed to leave, they were halfway through the second project and wanted to complete it.

If a sensor

painted a

canvas, it

would tend to

look like

a Norman

Rockwell.

If an

intuitive

painted a

canvas it

would tend

to look like

a Picasso.

## Complementary Styles

Can you begin to see how an S and an N might be attracted to one another? The staunch, staid, responsible one may admire the free-spirited butterfly. But can you also see the potential for driving each other up the wall after the infatuation and honeymoon bliss wear off?

S's are seen as rock-solid persons. N's are seen as creative. Their minds seem always to be in motion, figuring out things just for the fun of it. If an S painted a canvas, it would look like a Norman Rockwell. The canvas of an N would be more like a Picasso.

To illustrate the differences between a sensor and an intuitive, a class was divided into two groups based upon whether they were S's or N's. Each group was placed in a separate room with cans of Tinker Toys. The only instructions given were to make a building.

The building the S's made was precise and so strong that it could survive an 8.0 earthquake. But it was lacking style, beauty and creativity. To an intuitive it was too functional and even boring.

The building the intuitives created was a work of art. It was creative and would enrich the look of any city. But there was one problem. You could blow it over with one puff. There was no strength to the structure.

For the building to have had both beauty and strength, the S's and N's would have needed to work together.


### How the Differences Can Collide

The S person is a here-and-now individual. Dr. David Stoop and Jan Stoop share a choice example of this difference in the way an N and an S live life:

> Intuitive people do things quickly. They start down the hill and soon find a ski jump. As they fly through the air, they land at the bottom of the hill. It took them less than a minute to get there, and they sit down and wait for their sensing spouses. When those people arrive, the intuitive people ask them, "What on earth took you so long?" After the sensing people relate all they have seen on the way down the mountain, they stop and ask the intuitive people, "How did you get here?" Intuitive people can only say, "I don't know how, but I got here." Sensing people then reply, "It may take me longer, but at least I know how I got here." The sensing people see a lot of the details as well, whereas intuitive people are so quick to jump to a conclusion, they miss the details and sometimes miss out on the joy of the moment.[2]

Instead of accepting things at face value, N's want to probe deeper, always asking, "Why is it this way?" They can drive an S crazy with their inquisitive, speculative nature and with their general answers even to specific questions. It's difficult for others to follow an N's directions and instructions because there's a vague quality to them.

N's tend to see the forest rather than the individual trees, so specifics slip by them. On the other hand, even if they're sitting and looking at the forest, they may not see it because their minds are elsewhere.

The N and the S may be watching a TV show and the S will comment about something just seen. The N will say, "Where was that?" It was right there in front of them. But something the N saw triggered a thought that sent her mind careening off the subject to figure out and speculate about something else entirely. This is common and could happen when an S and an N are talking to one another. This is why an S may think his or her N spouse isn't listening.

## Differences in Handling Money

And then there are finances! An N balance the checkbook? What a chore. It's more intriguing to speculate how to spend the next paycheck. Money creates opportunities, and who knows what doors it can open for you? N's see the value of money in terms of its possibilities. They are drawn to investment opportunities because they see the possibility of making a lot of money, but they ignore the risk factor.

The way N's figure out how much money they have is intriguing. They're very adept at rounding off, either up or down! Some N's round down in their checking account any amount under $.50 and round up any amount over $.51. They have an exciting approach to money that may both intrigue and threaten an S.

## Differences in Expectations

N's tend to view relationships optimistically, at times even unrealistically. The subtle indications that a relationship is progressing are important—signs such as giving gifts and cards and remembering special dates. Change and variation in the relationship are very important. N's believe that the roles and expectations of a relationship are negotiable and open to change.[3] If you are an S, did you respond to dating in the same way? Probably not.

It's interesting to note the differences between S's and N's when it comes to dating. Perhaps you will remember this sequence. For an S a date begins when you get together. Not so for an N. A date can start when the first arrangements are made. They think and fantasize about the date and all the possibilities from that moment on. Once the date is over, they don't concentrate on that experience; they are already thinking about the next one. Actually, what occurs in an N's imagination is better than the real thing. On the second date the N might describe the first date in such a way that the S wonders if they were on the same date. Reality can become a bit distorted by the N's imagination.[4]

## What Do You Think?

1. Which of the previous characteristics fit you and which fit your spouse?
2. Can you describe a time when you had difficulty communicating because of the way the two of you are?

## Differences in Giving Directions

An S and an N differ greatly in the way they give directions. Let's apply the differences by showing how each type would instruct someone to follow a recipe. Here are the ingredients (as printed in a cookbook) for pumpkin soup:

| | |
|---|---|
| 1/2 lb. mushrooms, sliced | 1 T curry powder |
| 1 c. evap. milk | 1/2 c. chopped onions |
| 1# cooked, sieved pumpkin | dash nutmeg |
| 1 T butter | salt and pepper |
| 3 c. broth, vegetable or chicken | 1 T flour |
| 1 T honey | |

Here are the directions written to a sensor's specifications:

Lay out necessary equipment, including heavy pan, knife, caliper (please look this one up in a dictionary if you don't know what it is), thermometer, carpenter's level, tablespoons, measuring cups.

Be sure you check ingredients. Consult cookbook or call a friend to find out how much nutmeg is a dash and how much salt and pepper should go into a batch of pumpkin soup.

The mushrooms and onions need to be chopped (calipers will be helpful here—3/16-inch thickness recommended). Sauté mushrooms and onions in butter. After sautéing in butter, add one tablespoon flour. Why? This thickens the sauce a bit, preparatory to adding the liquids, and results in a thicker soup. You will know the mushrooms are cooked when a table knife encounters resistance when you try to cut one. You will know the onions are done when a table knife passes easily through.

Add flour. Add broth. (Be sure the measuring cup is on a level surface when you measure. Use a carpenter's level to be sure.) Add everything else except milk. Add milk, and heat without boiling. (Use a thermometer and don't let temperature rise above 200° F.) Serve in tureen and bowls pleasing to the eye, and garnish with chopped fresh parsley.

Here is how an intuitive might give the instructions (same ingredients):

There is a lot of possibility for creativity in this soup. A good, rich pumpkin soup offers potential for simultaneous cooking. Open your refrigerator. Now let your imagination roam. Water chestnuts, olives, a dab of mustard, some pieces of chicken. Whatever. If you are going to call this pumpkin soup, it might help to have some pumpkin, but mashed carrots, squash or even sweet potatoes will do. You might want to start by sautéing any ingredient that needs this process. In this way you will need to use only one pan. Add the rest of the ingredients and taste until it seems right to you.

While this soup heats (it is better not to boil it if you've included milk) you will probably want to make some rolls to go with the soup. While you're in the mood for cleaning the refrigerator and have to be in the kitchen anyway, you might want to defrost the freezer. In fact, you could get a little start on next week's cooking by frying up that frozen hamburger in the freezer. But the frying pan's dirty. That's OK because you'll be in the kitchen anyway, so you can wash the dishes.

And while you're washing dishes and thinking about the delicious soup on the stove, you can make plans either for a great soup-tasting event or for the restaurant you're going to open. Serve the soup in whatever is clean or send someone to the store for paper bowls.

Now, do you see how the differences between the two preferences play themselves out in everyday life? About 70 percent of
our population are sensors and 30 percent are intuitives.

## Accept the Differences

Remember than an S would prefer the N to respond more like an
S, and the N would prefer the S to respond more like an N. Don't
wait for the other person to take the first step. Be a model. Learn
to honor and respect your partner's uniqueness. Thank God for
the differences of your spouse. To do that you will need to do
two things: learn how to flex (and accomplish this to some
degree), but also let the other person just "be," realizing that he
or she is contributing something to you that you don't have.
Along that line, here are some things to consider.

If you're an S and your partner is an N, your partner will
challenge you with possibilities you've never considered. Be willing to consider them instead of immediately responding nega-
tively. Accept the fact that what the N does or says will probably
raise your anxiety over the risk factor involved.

Sometimes N's fail to notice something you've done for
them, what you've served them, or new clothes or furniture. Let
your N know that taking note and saying something is important to you. And if you're an N, make it a point to do so. You
might even write yourself a reminder note.

If you're an S, you're *not* responsible for the N's restlessness
or discontent. You haven't caused it and you can't fix it.

## Differences in Verbal Expression

An N can feel frustrated when an S isn't wildly enthusiastic
about some of his dreams and ideas. But an S may become

enthusiastic if the N presents the ideas in a simple and factual way and suggests that the S think about it. An S needs this type of communication in order to respond. Remember that your S partner will take care of the routing details you tend to overlook. Express your gratitude for this.[5]

An N needs to remember that what is said to an S will be taken at face value. In other words, taken literally. Do a reality check when you talk. Don't assume that what you said was what the S heard. An S will not distinguish between the facts (what you said) and what you actually meant.

S's tend to use complete sentences when they speak, and they end these sentences with a period. It's definite. Emphatic. N's tend to spin out sentences that omit information they assume the other person knows. They end the sentence with a dash. They are tentative. When these two types talk to one another, they listen to the other according to their specific trait and they assume the other person is talking in the same way they talk.

An S husband asks his N wife if she'd like to go away to the mountains for the weekend. She says, "No . . . I don't think so—" He assumes that since she said no, she meant it with a period. Not so! It was a dash. So when Friday comes, she asks her husband, "What time are we leaving for the mountains this weekend?"

He looks surprised and says, "What are you talking about? You said you didn't want to go!"

She replies, "I know I said that, but you should have known that's not what I meant. I needed to check on some things first, and I got them cleared up!"

Dr. David Stoop and Jan Stoop describe the intuitive mind as being in two parts. The intuitive person is aware of both parts but can't activate one of the parts. It's like an iceberg—10 percent is above the water where it can be seen; 90 percent is underwater. The part the intuitive can't articulate won't pop to the surface for a couple of days or until someone helps him articulate it. The Stoops write:

> It's important to know that you will never find out what the dash of the intuitive person means by asking a question. If that is what you do, you will simply get a rehash of the information that has already been given. Instead, the sensing person must paraphrase to the intuitive person what he or she heard the intuitive person say, and then allow the intuitive person to add to what has been said already. And this paraphrasing needs to be repeated until the intuitive person says, "Yes, that's what I've been trying to say to you."
>
> When intuitive people write out a first draft of a note or memo and then look at what they wrote, they will often add more information between the lines or up the side of the paper with an arrow to show where the thought goes. They do this because when they write they can see the part of the iceberg that is still underwater.[6]

Unfortunately, both S's and N's often assume their partners can read their minds. Major conflict is on the horizon unless these assumptions are dropped in favor of clarification. It may help after a discussion to ask, "Now, did you say that with a period or a dash?"

When an S talks, he or she usually identifies the topic and moves through it factually and sequentially, although a bit unimaginatively from an N's viewpoint. But an N may start talking without identifying the subject, then give three or four sentences of background material and go around the barn twice, because an N tends to be tangential in his thinking. Finally, the N arrives at the subject. Can you imagine what the S is doing all this time?

If you listen to two N's talking, sometimes neither person finishes a sentence, but both know exactly what the other is talking about. It's amazing!

If you're an S, you can feed an N's imagination by pointing out a possibility or by asking questions. I guarantee he or she will listen better. An S can learn to add more of the possibilities and details that an N desires. The first step is to remain calm. For example, when an N starts sharing but hasn't yet identified the topic, instead of getting frustrated, try to relax and realize that you're going to get the background information first. When the subject is finally identified, you'll have the entire picture. Although the delivery isn't the way you would like it, that's all right. Listening to an N's communication style will help you to become more flexible.

On the other hand, an N can work at identifying the subject in advance and letting his or her partner know the topic. If you're an N talking to an S, start with the details, and then build the big picture. Don't ramble; try to be as specific and factual as possible.

I'm an S and my wife, Joyce, is an N. (We can both access our nonpreferred side as well; after 40 years of marriage, you learn something.) Every now and then Joyce will come to me and look me in the eye and say, "OK. Here's the bottom line, Norm," and she'll give me a two-line factual summary. And we'll both laugh. On many occasions she will start without identifying the subject, give me three or four sentences of background material and then identify the topic. I've just learned to wait, because I'm getting the same information only in a different order. The subject is at the end. It's quite similar to sentence structure in the German language.

## Sensors and Intuitives in Prayer and Worship

Have you ever considered the differences in the way an S and an N respond in the spiritual dimension of life?

When sensors pray, they prefer specific prayer requests. They prefer a prayer list. Intuitives find a prayer list confining. When they pray they start on one topic, which suggests another topic and so on. Often their prayer life is very rich and elaborate.

When it comes to worship, sensors tend to be matter-of-fact. It doesn't have to be elaborate or fancy but should be simple and conducted in the proper manner. Intuitives want their worship experience to speak to the right side of the brain, not just instruct the left side. Teaching is all right, but inspiration is better.

How might the sensors in a worship service respond to a strong intuitive minister's preaching? How might an intuitive respond to a strong intuitive minister's preaching? How might the sensors in a worship service respond to a strong sensor minister's preaching? And how might an intuitive respond to the same?

In a Bible study, S and N differences are apparent. An S's approach is "read it, believe it, do it." A sensor doesn't like the idea that there might be secrets in the Scriptures and that we might have to figure out what God actually meant behind what was written. On the other hand, an N may want to find symbolism and secret meanings where there are none.

In a class situation, a sensor will ask precise questions and want the answers to be precise. N's want to see the possibilities of applying God's Word in many areas and in many ways.

If you and your spouse have the same preferences, each of you may want to work on accessing your opposite preference to bring more variety into your relationship as well as to learn how to communicate better with others in your lives.

## What's Your Plan?

1. Go back through the chapter and write down each characteristic that describes you. (You may find some characteristics on both sides of the fence.)
2. List how you will respond differently than you presently do and how you would like your spouse to respond differently.
3. Which characteristic about your spouse has been the most difficult for you to understand?

*Notes*
1. Otto Kroeger and Janet M. Thuesen, *Type Talk* (New York: Bantam Books, 1988), pp. 17, 18, adapted.
2. Dr. David Stoop and Jan Stoop, *The Intimacy Factor* (Nashville, Tenn.: Thomas Nelson Publishers, 1993), pp. 72, 73, adapted.
3. Sandra Hirsh and Jean Kummerow, *Life Types* (New York: Warner Books, 1989), pp. 30, 31, adapted.
4. Kroeger and Thuesen, *Type Talk*, p. 127, adapted.
5. David L. Luecke, *Prescription for Marriage* (Columbia, Md.: The Relationship Institute, 1989), pp. 58-60, adapted.
6. Stoop and Stoop, *The Intimacy Factor*, pp. 80, 81.

# DIFFERENT WAYS TO MAKE DECISIONS

—————————— CHAPTER TEN ——————————

Do you struggle when making decisions? Do you wonder why and how your partner makes decisions differently from the way you do? There are reasons for these differences that affect the way each of you communicates.

Some people are thinkers who make decisions quickly, while others are feelers who seem to take forever to reach a decision. The thinker style of communication tends to come across as sharp, clear, definite and decisive, while the feeler style tends to be cautious, gentle, investigative and option oriented.

This third set of MBTI preferences—thinker (T) or feeler (F)—shows how you and your partner individually prefer to make decisions. These differences will be quite evident in the communication process. For a relationship to succeed, you will need to mesh your differences and develop your own decision-making style as a couple.

Dr. David and Jan Stoop describe these two personality types:

Thinking people can stand back and look at the situation. They make a decision from an objective viewpoint, interpreting the situation from the outside. They believe that if they gather enough data they can arrive at the truth. They are always searching for this truth, which they believe exists as an absolute. These people see things as black and white—as absolutes. If the answer seems to lie in the gray area, thinking people believe they just haven't gathered enough data. If they can just look further, they will discover the truth.

On the other hand, feeling people always make decisions from a personal standpoint by putting themselves into the situation. They are subjective, believing that two truths can exist side-by-side.

The difference between a thinking person and a feeling person can be seen in the way the two make decisions, such as buying a car. Thinking people get the consumer reports and do research into different types of cars. They ask themselves, *Which is the best financial value? Which is safest?* They'll decide which criteria is most important to them and then make a decision based on that criteria. When they go to the car dealership, they'll know exactly what they want, and even that persuasive car salesman can't talk them into buying another car.

Feeling people start looking at all the cars on the road. *Which car would I like to be driving right now?* they ask themselves. *What color looks good? What make? What style?* When feeling people arrive at the car dealership, they may think, *I want a blue Honda coupe.* But after they've looked around a while, they may fall in love with a metallic green Honda Accord. And that's the car they'll purchase—even if it costs more money.

The important questions to ask yourself are: How do I make a decision? Do I listen more to my head when I make good decisions, or do I listen more to my heart?[1]

So, what about you? Do you listen more to your head or to your heart when you make decisions? What about your spouse?

## Using Your Head, Using Your Heart

The thinking or feeling preference is the trait that reflects how you *handle* your emotions, even though the trait really has very little to do with your emotions themselves. Thinkers (T) are often uncomfortable talking about feelings. They may also be uncomfortable in the areas of aesthetics and relationships. Other people may see them as aloof and cool, even though they actually are quite sensitive.

Feeling (F) individuals are comfortable with emotions. Not only are they aware of their own feelings, they can sense what others are experiencing as well. When it comes to making a decision, they're not just concerned with how it affects them but how it affects others as well.

To show you the difference, if a T were on a jury, he would be concerned with justice and fairness. He would look at the facts, find the truth and then make a decision. An F on a jury would be concerned with mercy. Facts are all right, but what were the circumstances? Why did the person do what he did? An F would want to give the benefit of the doubt.[2] (Who would you want on your jury?)

Do you have an idea yet where you stand on this? What about your spouse? Are you comfortable with each other's traits? How do your traits impact your communication with each other?

## The Thinker

If you're a thinker (T), you are the one who stays calm and collected in a situation where everyone else is upset. You keep your wits about you. You're the epitome of fairness when you make a decision. But you're not that concerned with what will make others happy. You are more firm minded than gentle minded. You want to make sure others know where you stand, whether they like it or not. You will state your beliefs rather than have others think they are right.

In fact, you're not concerned with whether people like you or not. What's important is being right. Your skin is quite thick. You can take it.[3] And argue? Sure—sometimes just for the fun of it. It's important for you to be objective even if others misinterpret you or your motives. And if you're also an E, how might this affect arguments? (Remember, an E believes one more statement would make things clear!)

If you're a T you enjoy making hard decisions and you can't understand why it's so difficult for others to do the same. Anything logical or scientific impresses you. You're drawn to it.

In your interpersonal relationships you may have difficulty remembering names. In a relationship, you need logical reasons for the purpose of the relationship's existence. You look at your partner not only in a realistic way but in a critical way, too. You tend to correct and try to redefine your partner. This can be expressed both verbally and nonverbally.

T's are reserved in the way they show love, and sometimes that expression is quite impersonal. They don't want to be out of control.

T's have a built-in filter to screen out the emotional parts of communication. It's uncomfortable for them to share their emotions. The simple but important niceties in a relationship are lacking.[4]

### The Feeler

If you're a feeler (F) you have a built-in antenna that picks up how others are feeling. And sometimes you allow them to dictate how you respond. You tend to overextend yourself to meet the needs of others, sometimes even if it costs you.

When you're trying to make a decision, you're always asking yourself, *How will this affect other people?* Sometimes you end up with a sense of tension—you like to help others but sometimes feel that you are always giving while others are taking. You may feel that others take advantage of you and that your own needs aren't being met.

If you are an F, you are well liked. Why? Because you're the peacemaker for everyone. "Let's all get along" is your motto. Sometimes others wonder if you have much of a backbone. You tend to change what you've said if you think it has offended someone.

You are very aware of your personal reasons for a relationship. You see the best in your partner and don't hold back expressions of love. You show your caring in a very personal way through words, cards, actions and so on. You're constantly scanning the other person's messages to see if there's any emotional meaning to the words. Any offering of emotional response is appreciated unless it's negative. You don't want anything to undermine your relationship.

## What Do You Think?

1. List any of the T characteristics that fit you.
2. List any of the F characteristics that fit you.

3. If you and your spouse are opposites, how has this affected your marriage?

The bonding material of a marriage is emotional intimacy.

This thinker/feeler preference is the only preference in which there is a gender distinction. Men make up 60 percent of T's and 40 percent of F's. Women make up 60 percent of F's and 40 percent of T's.

One writer describes the differences between a thinker and feeler by an event he once witnessed. He was attending a conference. During a break, the baby of one of the participants somehow became locked inside a closet.

The thinkers in the group responded to the problem in a task-oriented way, unaware of the emotional needs of the distraught baby's mother. Their take on the situation was, "We have a problem—a baby locked in a closet. Let's find a way to liberate it."

The feelers responded to the mother's emotional upset and tried to reassure her. They did what they did best—responded to a hurting person. They seemed so concerned for the mother that they seemingly had forgotten that someone needed to get the baby out of the closet.[5]

It's not uncommon for thinking people to intimidate feelers, because they can give reasons for their decisions. Feelers know what they believe to be right but usually say, "I just know it's right, but I can't give you the reason." Some T's are so into reasons that they won't consider something new unless the other person can give three reasons for it.

One of the most typical relationships that develops is between a male T and a female F. This connection has the most potential for creating divisiveness and long-term problems. T's need to think about and analyze their emotions. They bring to a marriage emotional control and reserve that can limit intimacy. They want to *understand* intimacy, not *experience* it, while an F wants to share openly and *experience* intimacy.

If a couple doesn't learn to connect emotionally, they're at risk for either an affair or a marriage breakup. The bonding material of a marriage is emotional intimacy. F's hunger for warmth, sharing and closeness, and without this dimension they can end up feeling lonely. They like the inner strength and security of a T but not the perceived emptiness.

Unfair as it sounds, a T will need to work more on adapting than will an F. Learning a vocabulary of intimacy and how to describe emotions is essential. A T's uniqueness is definitely needed but can create a sterile relationship. T's and F's are attracted by each other's differences but at the same time are a bit repelled by them. A T desires intimacy but could fear it even more.[6]

Feelers need to work on being less subjective and feeling less responsible for everyone's emotional state. They need to take things less personally and learn to become assertive and face disagreements. They need to stop saying "I'm sorry" and "It's my fault" so much.

A thinker takes care of things; a feeler takes care of people. A thinker takes care of organization; a feeler provides warmth and harmony. A thinker brings emotional control to a relationship; a feeler provides emotional energy.

# What Do You Think?

1. What can you do to access your nonpreference side? How might this enrich your life?
2. If one of you is a T and the other an F, how could you improve your communication?

## Working on Compatibility

Can a T and an F be compatible in marriage? Yes, but it will take constant work. Each partner must avoid judging the other for the way he or she is wired and realize that neither partner will ever become just like the other; you can defeat yourself and put a strain on your relationship by trying to make your partner think like you. Sure, a T wants the F to be more analytical and efficient and get to the point quicker. And the F wants the T to show more transparency, emotional expression and social awareness. Both of you can learn to accommodate these desires to a point. This is what is meant by learning to become compatible.

Both parties must remember they were initially attracted to each other because of who they are. View your partner's uniqueness as a gift and a plus for you. The fact is, each of you is incomplete without the other. You are a gift to each other.

A thinker takes care of things, and a feeler takes care of people.

A thinker takes care of organization, and a feeler provides warmth and harmony.

A thinker brings emotional control to a relationship, while a feeler provides emotional energy.

A thinker gives structure; a feeler nurtures.

If you're a T, stretch yourself to enter into the social life provided by your F partner. Watch and listen to how F's interact. When you're talking to an F, be more expressive and tentative and use feeling words. You'll gain more friends that way. Accept the way your F partner shares. Praise your partner for her feelings and tell her you need to learn what she has to offer.

Be realistic and accept the fact that you probably won't be able to satisfy all your F partner's relational needs. Encourage and support her long, feeling conversations on the phone and her same-sex relationships. Don't force her to cut back on her friendships.

If you're an F, remind yourself of the qualities of your T partner and note how you make use of his T characteristics. You will need his problem-solving abilities. He will add energy, organization and direction to your spontaneity.

Here are some guidelines for both T's and F's to follow when talking with each other. If you're an F, here's how to communicate with your T spouse:

**Explain yourself clearly, logically and concisely.** Thinkers often want to know the why. Give them the reasons before they ask for them.

**Define your terms.** For an F, the statement "I love you" doesn't need any definition. It speaks for itself. For a T, the same simple statement can mean a number things.

**Listen for what a T says before attempting to interpret how he has said it.**

If you're a T, here's what you can do when you're talking to your F spouse:

**Provide plenty of verbal affirmation.** Most F's thrive on praise and encouragement.

**Don't underestimate the value of small talk.** To most F's there is no such thing as small talk. When they share their day with you, they aren't just downloading a list of data; they're giving you a part of themselves.

**Don't listen to how logical an F's reasons are when talking; listen for what they are feeling**. Ask questions that draw them out.

F's must remember that T's simply cannot fulfill all their social or relational needs. Don't interpret his cool reserve as personal rejection but as a personality trait. What may hurt you probably wasn't intended to hurt you. You may need to guide a T, in a positive manner, in new ways to express things to you. But that's what relationships are all about—growth.[7]

Remember that both of you are a mixture of T and F. One trait is dominant in each of you, so both of you may need to work on nurturing (I used a feeling word because I'm an F) your less dominant preference.

By the way, when you pray for your partner, do you thank God for the fact that he or she is either a T or an F? And speaking of prayer, when a T prays, he or she will probably reflect on the attributes of God. For them Bible study is a time to study the doctrinal and ethical truths of their faith. A feeler spends more time with his or her heavenly friend. For a feeler, knowing *about* God is all right, but knowing God *personally* is so much better. In a Bible study, feelers want to be moved emotionally.

## What Do You Think?

1. Describe how your preference is demonstrated in the expression of your faith, your prayer life and your worship style.

## How Do You Approach Life?

There is one last set of preferences in the *Myers-Briggs Type Indicator*—Judging (J) and Perceiving (P). Let's consider this set of preferences through a scenario that typifies each viewpoint:

### The Judger

You're out to dinner at a restaurant and there's a couple sitting next to you. The waiter comes up to take the order and the wife says, "I'll have the rib-eye cut, medium rare, baked potato with butter only and the salad with dressing on the side." The waiter asks, "What kind of dressing? We have French, blue cheese, honey mustard, Italian and ranch." She replies, "Ranch."

The waiter turns to the man, and the man asks several questions. He wants to know the differences among several of the steaks and which is the most popular. (By the way, this couple eats here regularly.) He looks around at several tables to see what others are eating. After all this, he seems to have enough information to select a meal. He orders fish. Then he asks what salad dressings are available (even though the waiter already listed them when the wife ordered). Just as the waiter starts to walk away, the man changes his mind and orders a steak.

Have you been around a couple like this? Perhaps it describes you and your spouse.

The last MBTI category—J or P—measures how you like to live your life. Do you like structure and organization, or is your approach to life free-flowing, spontaneous and adaptive? People whose preference is for structure are called judgers, while free-form types are perceivers.

This preference largely determines what you share when you begin to talk, and it is critical to the communication process. Let's consider this in your steps to becoming compatible with your partner.

If you're a J, you're extremely conscious of time and schedules. It's as though you have a built-in clock. You seem to spend a good portion of your life waiting for others who don't have a clear understanding of time. This can be a big source of irritation to you, especially if you're an SJ.

You're also a list keeper. You're probably one of those persons who has a Day-Timer and who makes it work. Crossing off listed items gives you great satisfaction. Your entire day is mapped out from the time you wake up until bedtime. If something interferes with your schedule, watch out.

In school you probably completed assigned projects in advance. You like order, from the way things are arranged in the cupboard to the color-coded clothes hanging a half-inch apart in the closet.

Your motto is "Get the work done first; then play." If you have a task to do, you'll keep at it until it's done, even if waiting would give you better resources to do a better job.

J's view interruptions and surprises as totally unnecessary. People around them soon learn that the best way to tell a J about a change in routine is to tell him, then leave for 10 minutes to let the J fuss and get it out of his system, and then come back and discuss it.

In order to be spontaneous, a J has to plan it in advance!—"A week from Sunday I will be spontaneous from 1:00 to 5:00 P.M."

When you talk, you economize on words. You give decisions but don't always provide enough data to back up the decisions. (What might you be like if you are a J as well as an S and a T?) It's important to begin to notice the grouping of these traits and what that means. At the conclusion of this chapter are reading resources, if you want to learn more about how to interpret the traits.

J's think of money as something that provides security. It's one of the ways to measure their success and progress. The best thing to do with money? Save it. This means investing wisely, budgeting, being careful in giving it away, prioritizing how to spend it and using it for your child's college and your retirement. How might this trait affect the communication in your marriage?

How do judgers relate in a marriage relationship? They may want to set up actual time periods to work on the relationship. They tend to put off the playful part of a relationship until work is out of the way. They know that one of the best ways to build a marriage is to work on it together. They're comfortable with doing things traditionally, or by the book.

## The Perceiver

Who do you think a J is often attracted to? You're right—a perceiver (P). But talk about opposites! The perceiver loves adventure—the unknown is there to be explored, even if it's finding alternative routes home each day. If you're a perceiver, planning is not for you. It's too limiting. You would rather wait and see what unfolds.

Those who see you as disorganized just don't understand you. Neatness has little appeal for you. Sure, you would like to be organized, but that's not nearly as important as being creative, spontaneous and responsive. A pile of papers to a J is nothing more than a mess to clean up. But to a P, that pile of papers is like compost. If you leave it there long enough, something good is bound to happen! Can you see how these characteristics both intrigue a J and frustrate him as well?

Time. What is time to a P? Even if you have a watch you don't look at it or want to be limited by it. You wait until the last minute to get things done, and although you usually get them done, you upset others in the process. In school you probably pulled an all-nighter to get that paper done or to prepare for an exam.

As a P, your attention span is extremely flexible. That's another way to say you're easily distracted. Things have to be fun. If someone tells you a work project will be fun, you respond in a positive way. Just as possibilities are so important to the N, fun is critical to the P.

It's difficult for you to make up your mind about things. If you do, it may limit you from doing something better that might come along. Others may see you as noncommittal, hesitant or not having the ability to make up your mind.

You may come home with clothes from the store but take them back the next day because you'll find something better at another store. Acting in a definite way is not your forte. You don't want to rule out anything by deciding one way or another.

A P's motto for conversation is "I'll get around to it" or "It's around here somewhere." (The word "ramble" comes to mind.) A P can jump from one subject to another and the topic may be something he or she just saw through the window or recently watched on a TV show.

As a P, you are agile and flexible in your conversation style. You don't need to resolve your discussions, even though you may go around the barn three or four times. When you make a point, you may say it several different ways. It's as though you get paid by the word. But sometimes you're so vague that it's hard to follow your train of thought. If you're also an extrovert, everyone will hear you change your thoughts in the middle of a sentence and even interrupt yourself. And if you're an N . . . ! Think of all the possibilities! What fun!

It's an amazing experience for others to hear you talking with another P because the conversation can go anywhere and in all directions at one time. You may not finish your sentence before moving on, but the other P follows you. (A J wouldn't be able to follow.) If the person is an NP, what might his or her communication style be like?

Then there's the way a P looks at finances: Money is a means to help you get the most out of life. The best way to use it is *spend it!* Ask P's what to do with money and you hear responses such as, "Have fun with it"; "Enjoy it when you have it"; "If you see someone in need, give them some"; "Take a trip on the spur of the moment"; "Take some friends on a cruise."[8]

Perceivers experience some tension when considering commitment. They're more hesitant because they don't want to cut off options. Sometimes they're up and down over the status of their relationships. When they do commit, it's still open for reevaluation.

Where a J wants security, a P wants freedom. This tendency is also seen in regard to activities on the social calendar. Come what may, a J wants to keep the appointment; but a P will say, "I may go, and then again, something else may come up that interests me more."

If there's work to do on the relationship, P's typically want to wait and deal with it when an issue arises. They will look for ways to combine work and play. P's prefer to be creative, to let it flow and to see what develops.[9]

## What Do You Think?

1. Do you know someone who fits the J description? The P description?
2. What conflicts might arise between a J and P couple?
3. What conflicts would two J's experience if married to one another? What conflicts would two P's experience?

## J's and P's in Marriage

How will you develop your compatibility as a J married to a P? Here is what Dr. David Stoop and Jan Stoop say:

Judging and perceiving organizers complement each other's styles. Judging people are sometimes tired of living in their structured, organized world and would love to break free. As they watch the play ethic of the perceiving person, they long for that fun-loving approach to life. During the early stages of a relationship, they will often act a lot like the perceiving person, in that they will drop what they are doing and have some fun.

On the other hand, perceiving people get frustrated with always organizing and never actually being organized. They sometimes long for some structure in their lives or for someone who will be decisive and know where to put things. During the early stages of the relationship, they may even feel a spurt of organizational skill that puts some structure in their lives.

Judging people want some freedom from structure, but not that much freedom. If things get too flexible they begin to feel as if their lives are unraveling and they are losing control, so they quickly go back to their strength and tighten the loose ends.

Perceiving people may look to their partner to help them get organized but will begin to feel crowded by the seemingly endless structures and start to loosen things up a bit.

One judging husband, who later admitted that what attracted him to his perceiving wife was her playful spirit, wanted to help her get organized. One weekend, when she was away visiting her family, he decided to make it easier for her to organize her kitchen. He emptied all the cupboards and the pantry and cleaned it all meticulously, and then put in new white shelf paper. As he put everything back into the cupboards, he took a black marker and made the shape of the item on the shelf-paper. Inside one circle he wrote "peanut butter." In a rectangle, he wrote "cereal." He couldn't wait for her appreciative response. After all, he was helping her get organized.

Little did he imagine the intensity of her reaction. She was livid! She took it as the ultimate insult. And for her it was, for he was saying that her personality style was inadequate, that she needed help. It didn't take very long for her to put the peanut butter where he had written "cereal" and the dishes over the word "glasses."

Unfortunately, this husband had lost sight of his appreciation of his wife's personality. When pressed, he could identify how much he enjoyed her spontaneity, her ability to manage a large number of things at one time and her fun-loving spirit.

You might think that only judging people are perfectionists. The truth is that both types struggle with perfectionism. Perceiving organizers think they're great organizers, but if you ask them whether they can keep their files organized they have to say no. They're always in a hurry to get on to something else so they don't keep their things organized. Judging people are practicing perfectionists, and perceiving people are practicing perfectionists.[10]

Often you hear a J saying to a P, "The problem with you P's is that you answer a question with another question." The perceiver responds, "So . . . is that bad?"

If you are a J or a P trying to connect with your opposite, consider the strength each of you brings to the relationship. A P is the one who expands information and alternatives before making decisions. Some of these alternatives could be better than what the J partner has considered. On the other hand, the J will make sure that conclusions are reached and decisions followed.

Each of you will need to allow more time in order to hear what the other person has to say. Don't immediately think the other is wrong or try to convince him that you are right. Don't engage in labeling. (P's tend to call J's close-minded, opinionated and stubborn; J's are tempted to label P's as flaky, unsupportive or wishy-washy.)

J's can encourage P's to take more time, to consider alternatives and to change their minds. It helps if a J uses the word "fun" in what he or she suggests to a P. J's can also work on being less definite and emphatic when they make statements. They can give in to the other person and, instead of always giving advice or conclusions, ask a question.

J's can give their P partners more responsibility for planning and decisions. And don't expect a P to immediately back a J's decisions. He or she needs time to explore. Don't back a P into a corner by predetermining responses and solutions. J's must stretch their ability to live with indecision, unanswered questions and things being out of control.

If you are a J, remember that there is more than one right answer. Don't take a P's seeming lack of commitment and support personally. P's have a different timetable and intensity. Remember, their motto is "I'll get around to it," and even that will be voiced tentatively.

Every now and then, both of you, J and P alike, should purposefully do things the way the other does them. It will help you both to flex, and you may be surprised that you can do it.[11]

## More Ways to Speak Each Other's Language

Thank each other for the way both of you are wired. You need what the other has to offer, even though you may feel threatened by the differences.

If you're a P, above all, make every effort to be on time when you have told your J partner a specific time. We live in a society that puts value on punctuality. If necessary, write yourself reminder notes and place them where you can see them easily and frequently.

Sometimes P's think they can get "just these four tasks" completed before they leave, which contributes to being late. The way to overcome this is to come up with the four things you think you can do, and then do just one or two of them. That way you can feel good that you accomplished at least a couple of things and can still be on time. Perhaps you need to begin seeing yourself as a person who *is* on time!

As a P, be more definite when you share how you feel about your partner. Let him know you're not challenging his decisions; you just need time to explore on your own. Keep in mind that what your J partner is saying may not be set in concrete, even if he says it is. Ask your partner how important the decision is, on a scale of 0 to 10; if it's anything more than a 6, follow through on it.

If you tend to drift off the topic in a conversation and your J partner brings you back to the issue at hand, thank him for doing so. You probably needed that.[12]

Remember that your J partner's need for certainty and structure is who he is, not a personal vendetta to control you.

Some couples believe they have an ideal relationship because they both have the same set of preferences on the *Myers-Briggs Type Indicator*. Perhaps . . . but maybe not. The combination of your preferences does affect your marriage, but both the preferences you have and the ones you don't have help determine the quality of your relationship.

You may have a complementary advantage when you have the same preference as your spouse, but you will lack the advantage of the preference you're missing. For example, if both of you are missing a certain preference, you would probably avoid the activities or experiences enjoyed by someone with that preference. To enjoy the full spectrum of the personality preferences you would have to make an effort to access your nonpreference side and learn to use it. You would need to read as much as you could about the missing preference and learn to compensate for what you don't have.

Remember: You do not, will not and cannot change your spouse's personality type. You learn to adjust to it. There is no wrong personality type. It is God's gift to each person. Yet the bridge between the personalities in marriage partners may need to be relocated a bit for better traffic flow.

Why not make some 3x5 cards with the following statements and read them over several times a day to reinforce how God sees you and your spouse (see 1 Cor. 6:19,20; 1 Peter 1:18,19; Rev. 5:9).

1. My personality is God's gift to me.

2. I am made in the image of God.

3. God loves me very much.

4. I am worth the precious blood of Jesus; my spouse is worth the precious blood of Jesus.

## What's Your Plan?

1. Go back through the chapter and write down each characteristic that describes you. (You may find some characteristics in both preferences that describe you.)
2. List how you can respond differently and how you would like your spouse to respond differently.

3. Which characteristic about your spouse has been the most difficult for you to understand?

4. Write out what you and your spouse have learned up to this point about your communication styles.

5. To what extent are you now speaking your spouse's language style?

| 0 | 5 | 10 |
|---|---|---|
| Are you kidding? | Average | Yes! |
| | | We're there! |

Here are a couple of resources to help you learn more about your personality type:

*Type Talk* by Otto Kroeger and Janet M. Thuesen
*Why Can't I Be Me?* by Mark A. Pearson

*Notes*

1. Dr. David Stoop and Jan Stoop, *The Intimacy Factor* (Nashville, Tenn.: Thomas Nelson Publishers, 1993), pp. 88, 89.
2. Stoop and Stoop, *The Intimacy Factor,* pp. 90, 91, adapted.
3. Otto Kroeger and Janet M. Thuesen, *Type Talk* (New York: Bantam Books, 1988), pp. 18, 19, adapted.
4. David L. Luecke, *Prescription for Marriage* (Columbia, Md.: The Relationship Institute, 1989), pp. 44, 45, adapted.
5. Mark A. Pearson, *Why Can't I Be Me?* (Grand Rapids, Mich.: Chosen Books, 1992), p. 42, adapted.
6. Luecke, *Prescription for Marriage,* pp. 64, 65, adapted.
7. Ibid., pp. 64-69, adapted.
8. Kroeger and Thuesen, *Type Talk,* pp. 21, 22, adapted.
9. Ibid., pp. 21, 22; Otto Kroeger, *16 Ways to Love Your Lover* (New York: Delacorte Press, 1994), pp. 86, 87, adapted.
10. Stoop and Stoop, *The Intimacy Factor,* pp. 112-115, adapted.
11. Luecke, *Prescription for Marriage,* pp. 71, 72, adapted.
12. Kroeger, *16 Ways to Love Your Lover,* p. 97, adapted.

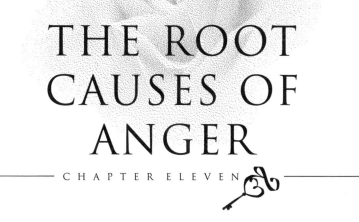

# THE ROOT CAUSES OF ANGER

CHAPTER ELEVEN

The discussion started out quite innocently. They were sitting at the kitchen table on a Saturday morning, drinking a cup of coffee and looking forward to a leisurely day. No projects, no obligations and no pressure, for a change. They laughed occasionally and talked about their vacation plans for the next month. The atmosphere was light and pleasant.

An hour later their voices had climbed to a shrill height. Anger flashed in their eyes. The words they spoke came out as if they could be hurled at one another.

What happened? Why the change in this peaceful atmosphere? The discussion about their vacation had raised some differences of opinion—a minor problem that could easily have been worked out but instead had ignited a spark of anger in one spouse that quickly spread to the other. The day was ruined, the coffee tasted terrible now, and there would be no resolution of the vacation plans this day.

Anger is a baffling emotion. Although it is a God-given emotion, most of the time when people get angry, the results are negative: anger is the second major cause of automobile accidents in our country; it is involved in the bruised and battered bodies of millions of children and spouses in our nation; it is sometimes the cause of failed marriages when one or both marriage partners do not use it constructively. When anger penetrates a discussion or conflict, it's difficult to come to an acceptable resolution.

## What Is Anger?

If I were to ask what anger means to you, what would you say? Do you have a definition for anger? You know what it feels like, but can you define it?

Simply put, anger is a strong feeling of displeasure and irritation. But anger can soon take a downhill slide into other emotional responses such as rage, fury or even wrath. Wrath is fervid anger looking for vengeance. Rage is an intense, uncontained, explosive response.

When anger erupts into conflict and goes unresolved, rage and resentment may begin to emerge.

Rage drives a person to destroy, to take revenge. It uses open warfare. Resentment breeds bitterness and often creates passive-aggressive responses. It's a feeling of indignant displeasure or a persistent ill will against an insult, an injury or a feeling of being wronged. When you resent someone, you create a filter through which you view that person. You become a flaw finder; blame is now a major response toward your partner. Often feelings of resentment result in guerrilla warfare tactics—hitting and running when your partner is least likely to suspect an attack.

Does this description of rage and resentment reveal anything about its effectiveness or lack of effectiveness for resolving conflicts and building harmony in a marriage? As Richard Walters puts it, "Rage blows up the bridges people need to reach each other, and resentment sends people scurrying behind barriers to hide from each other and to hurt each other indirectly."[1]

The danger of anger is even indicated by the various ways people try to deal with it. Some people pretend they have no anger and bury it. But what they bury is alive and in time will tend to destroy them through ulcerated colitis, depression or even a stroke. Anger that is buried is kept alive in the mind.

Some people vent by letting out all their anger. They've heard it's healthy. But this misinformation alienates their spouse, employer and friends, and soon there is no one around to vent their anger upon. Most people feel worse after venting anger; immediately afterward they feel more irritable, depressed, aggravated, hostile, jittery and unhappy. Others turn anger on themselves and begin to destroy their self-esteem, their identity and their capabilities.

Anger becomes a problem when it takes the form of two extremes: overreaction or underreaction. When we underreact, we repress or suppress our anger, often without realizing what we're doing. When we choose to block it out, we are not being honest with ourselves or those around us.

When we overreact, our anger is out of control. It comes out in rage and fury, which can lead to violence. I have seen the dark blue bruises on a face or the wince when someone touches the injured area of a person's body. But that pain is minor compared to the inner emotional pain. Skin bruises eventually turn back to their normal color, but the inner discoloration lasts much longer.

## The Truth About Anger

Let's explore some truths about anger. Hold on, because what I'm going to say may sound contrary to what you have believed about this emotion.

Anger is not the problem or the main emotion; it is a symptom.

Expressing your anger to your partner does not lessen your anger; it usually increases it.

How you use your anger is a learned response. This means that you can learn a new response and get your anger under control.

Your partner is not responsible for making you angry—you are!

How do you feel after reading these statements? Angry? Confused? Upset? Amazed? Let's consider what you've just read. Remember: What you do with the information in this chapter can have a dramatic affect on the amount of harmony and satisfaction you experience in your marriage.

## Anger's Root Causes

Anger is what we call a secondary emotion. It is a message system telling you that something else is happening inside you. Anger is caused by fear, hurt or frustration. That's right—fear, hurt or frustration.

## Fear

You may be afraid that your partner is going to override you, control you, yell at you, be unreasonable, not give you what you want, verbally attack you, withdraw, ignore you and so on. To protect yourself from your fear, you attack with anger.

Whenever you begin to experience anger, ask yourself, *Am I afraid of something right now? What am I feeling?* You may discover the cause right at that moment. Try telling your partner, "I feel somewhat fearful right now. Could we talk about it? I would rather do that than become angry."

## Hurt

Hurt comes from many causes—a sharp word, cooking a fine meal and its being passed over, painting the house and not receiving an appreciative comment, being slapped, discovering an affair and so on. To relieve our hurt we become angry. We want the other person to pay. We want to even the score. But hurting people do not keep score in the same way. When we've been hurt, we don't always want to admit the extent of the hurt, so we cover it over with anger.

When you are angry, ask yourself, *Am I feeling hurt? Where is this hurt coming from?* In place of your anger, try telling your partner, "Right now I'm really feeling hurt. I wanted to let you know, and talk about it and not have it develop into anger."

## Frustration

Frustration is at the heart of much of our anger. The word "frustration" comes from the Latin *frustra*, which means "in vain." We are frustrated when we confront a problem but can't find a solution for it. Frustration is the experience of walking into dead-end

Give your

partner

permission to

talk the way

he or she

does, to

do things

differently

from you,

to be late,

to be silent.

I guarantee

your

frustration

will

lessen.

streets and blind alleys and getting nowhere.

A common myth is that frustration always has to upset us. It doesn't! If your partner is talking or acting in a way that bothers you, you may feel frustrated, but you can control your response both inwardly and outwardly. Many of your spouse's behaviors and reactions will not be what you would want. From time to time we all tend to magnify what the other person has done and literally create a mountain out of a molehill.

There are hundreds of little annoyances that can activate the frustration button, but these annoyances are part and parcel of married life. Accepting them and giving them permission to be there can relieve some of the pressure. Give your partner permission to talk the way he or she does, to do things differently from you, to be late, to be silent. I guarantee your frustration will lessen! Why? Because you have brought yourself back under control. We frequently become frustrated when we feel out of control.

Resist the temptation to act aggressively when you get frustrated. It's a normal tendency to act out, but it's like blowing your horn at a train stopped on the tracks in front of you because the train is making you late to your destination. It's futile!

Remember, it isn't your partner who makes you angry. It's your inner response to the person that creates the anger. You and you alone are responsible for your emotions and reactions.

### Practicing a Better Response to Anger

Let me be facetious for a minute and suggest how you can make yourself angry at your spouse. It's quite easy. Just do the following. Suppose you're having a discussion with your spouse, and you approach him or her with the attitude that you want something and must have it. The key words are "want" and "must." The next step after not getting what you want is to say, "This is terrible. It's awful not to get what I want. Why don't you see it my way?" Then you say, "You shouldn't frustrate me like this. I must have my way. How dare you! You'll pay for this!" Then the blame game begins. When we think we must have our way, the frustration begins to build.

Janice shared with me an experience that happened just two days before her appointment with me. She described how she had spent six hours cleaning the house from corner to corner and top to bottom. She literally slaved over each room, making it spotless. She was hoping for some appreciation and response from her husband. Unfortunately, he came home tired, hungry and looking forward to the Monday-night football game on TV. Not a word of appreciation did he say, nor did he seem to notice what she had done. In fact, in a half hour he had undone much of her work in the family room by spreading himself and his stuff all over the furniture. We began talking about her thoughts that led up to the tirade and the blowup that lasted from 9:00 to 11:30 that night. Here's what she came up with:

"He should have noticed all the work I did today!"

"He should have thanked me for what I did."

"He shouldn't have been so insensitive and inconsiderate."

"What a louse he is! He has no class or sensitivity."

"Look at him! He messes up all my work!"

"He'll probably want sex tonight. Just wait. He'll pay for this and sleep by himself!"

We then talked about each statement and how it made her feel. Soon she began to see how her statements created feelings of hurt, frustration, rejection and anger. The rest of the session was spent on developing some realistic responses to what had happened. As we brainstormed together about how to handle a disappointing experience, Janice began making a list. Here are some of the responses she could have used:

"I wish he had noticed all my work."

"I wonder why it's so important to have John notice the work and thank me for it. Did I do this for him, for me or for . . . ?"

"Perhaps I could find a creative way to share with him what I did today. I could bring in the camera and ask him if he would like to take a picture of a fantastically clean house and the housekeeper who created this wonder!"

We then formulated a summary statement that helped to put everything in perspective for her. It went like this: "I want John to notice the clean house I've spent six hours slaving over today. But if he doesn't, that's all right, too. My happiness and sense of satisfaction doesn't depend on his response. I didn't clean it up just for his response. I cleaned it because it needed to be cleaned. I feel good about my effort and how it turned out. His appreciation would just be an added benefit."

Is there something in your own life that would be helped by a response such as this? Perhaps you've experienced a recent frustration. Recall what you said to yourself and then formulate a new statement that would have lowered your frustration. It works!

## A Biblical Response to Anger

Do you know what this process actually does? It helps you put into practice some wisdom that can change your relationships with others. The Bible gives us several directives and thoughts about this emotion called anger.

> Let all bitterness and indignation and wrath (passion, rage, bad temper) and resentment (anger, animosity) and quarreling (brawling, clamor, contention) and slander (evil-speaking, abusive or blasphemous language) be banished from you, with all malice (spite, ill will or baseness of any kind) (Eph. 4:31, *AMP*).

In this verse, Paul is referring to anger as a turbulent emotion that boils up within us.

The Christian is also to put away anger that is abiding and habitual, the kind of anger that seeks revenge:

> But now put away and rid yourselves [completely] of all these things: anger, rage, bad feeling toward others, curses and slander, and foulmouthed abuse and shameful utterances from your lips! (Col. 3:8, *AMP*).

Scripture teaches us not to provoke others to anger:

The terror of a king is as the roaring of a lion; whoever provokes him to anger or angers himself against him sins against his own life (Prov. 20:2, *AMP*).

The Bible directs us to be "slow to anger" (that is, to control our anger) and to be careful of close association with others who are constantly angry or hostile.

A hot-tempered man stirs up strife, but the slow to anger pacifies contention (Prov. 15:18).

He who is slow to anger is better than the mighty, he who rules his [own] spirit than he who takes a city (Prov. 16:32, *AMP*).

Make no friendships with a man given to anger, and with a wrathful man do not associate, lest you learn his ways and get yourself into a snare (Prov. 22:24,25, *AMP*).

Scripture also speaks of justified anger. An example is found in the life of the Lord Jesus:

And He glanced around at them with vexation and anger, grieved at the hardening of their hearts, and said to the man, Hold out your hand. He held it out, and his hand was [completely] restored (Mark 3:5, *AMP*).

In Ephesians 4:26 (*AMP*) the apostle Paul speaks of two kinds of anger and how to deal with both:

When angry, do not sin; do not ever let your wrath (your exasperation, your fury or indignation) last until the sun goes down.

In the phrase "when angry, do not sin," Paul is describing the kind of anger that is an abiding, settled attitude against sin and sinful things. You are aware that you are angry and you're in control of your anger. In this verse, God is actually instructing us to be angry about the right thing! Anger is an emotion created by God; He created us as emotional beings. The phrase "do not sin" is a check against going too far. The kind of anger that is justified because it is against sin and sinful things and fully under your control is the kind of anger that has God's approval.

In the phrase "do not ever let your wrath . . . last until the sun goes down," Paul is speaking of another meaning for anger. Here he links anger to irritation, exasperation and embitterment. As Ephesians 4:31 and Colossians 3:8 instruct us to do, we are supposed to put this kind of anger away. If we do get angry in this negative sense, we should deal with it quickly—before sundown. Scripture counsels us never to take irritation or embitterment to bed. If we do we are sure to lose sleep (not to mention peace, friends and even our health).

## What Do You Think?

1. Using the biblical descriptions of anger, describe the kind of anger you usually experience. How do you express anger?

2. Describe the kind of anger your spouse usually seems to experience. How does your spouse usually express this anger?

3. What can a person do to become "slow to anger"?

4. Describe how a person can be angry and not sin.

As we see from the verses we've read, not all anger is wrong. Write down some of the verses—especially from the book of Proverbs—on some 3x5 cards and keep them with you. Read them aloud several times a day for a month. By that time the verses will be committed to memory. Then the Holy Spirit has the opportunity to bring them back to your conscious memory when you need them, and your anger responses can be consistent with the Word of God.

When you begin to experience anger, ask yourself, *What am I frustrated about? What am I doing to frustrate myself? Do I have some expectations, needs or wants that are not being met? Does my partner know what they are? Are these needs, wants or expectations necessary? Do I have to be frustrated at this time?* If you take the time to answer these questions, it will make a difference in your life.

## The Blame Game

Blame is the core issue of anger. You blame your partner when you find fault with the person and what he or she has done. Blame looks to accuse, point the finger, find fault, criticize, reproach, berate, disparage, chide, take to task.

Will blame accomplish what you want? Will it bring you closer to your mate? Will it reflect the presence of Jesus Christ in your life and in your marriage? Blame seeks to make the other person aware of what he or she has done and in some cases to make the person pay. But if we place blame, he or she may continue to do the same behavior but with greater intensity. Some of the worst statements and descriptions are those thrown at a person during the heat of anger. If your partner is especially sensitive, he or she may end up believing your words.

We blame others with the hope of correcting what they have done. How sad! How futile! How self-defeating! When you blame, you trigger your partner's defense system and push him or her into greater anger, making the person want to fight you. If the justification process we use isn't working, then we think anger is the next best alternative. Blame does not help anger go away, and it distracts you from discovering a solution to your frustration.

## The Best Alternative to Blame

The New Testament has something far better to offer than blame. It is called forgiveness, and it works. Forgiveness relieves us of the tremendous pressure of attempting to make others pay for what they have done to us—even a spouse. Blame makes a person ill; forgiveness makes a person well.

## Expressing Anger Appropriately

Earlier I mentioned that expressing anger doesn't necessarily make it disappear. Let's look at the myths of getting anger out of our systems.

In many marital arguments we find the following scenario: the problem erupts and there is an angry outburst and verbal attacks, which may include screaming and crying, exhaustion, a sullen apology and a strained relationship for several days. Is this helpful? Does it resolve the conflict? I'm not suggesting that we bottle up all our anger or repress it. But the way in which most individuals ventilate their anger does not make it disappear. Often when we verbally express our anger at our partner, we say things that are hard to forget. We're more concerned about proving the other person wrong or controlling him or even punishing him.

An interesting study was conducted with divorced women to discover the cause of growth or stagnation. Two hundred fifty-three women were interviewed twice—once during the upsetting time of divorce and then again four months later. Many questions were used to discover attitudes and reactions: Did you show your anger or keep it in? Did you recover from it quickly or slowly?

The women who let anger out were *not* in better shape than those who kept it in. Expressing anger did not automatically make a woman feel better, and it did not improve the woman's self-esteem. Those whose mental health improved were those who had an active social life following the divorce and *did not* harp on the divorce. Those who did not grow also socialized but tended to talk obsessively about the divorce.[2]

I'm not suggesting that we should never talk about our anger or let it out. But we need to choose a way to express it that will cause the anger to go away. Only then are we free from its tyranny over our life and marriage. Anger can be positive if it helps us solve the cause of the anger. We need to communicate our anger without condemning! We need to express it in a way that reduces the anger and draws us closer to our partner. How do we do that?

## How to Navigate Conflict

First, let's consider what you can do when your spouse is upset or angry with you. Remember, just because the other person is angry doesn't mean that you have to become angry. Here are some suggestions.

### Accept Your Spouse's Emotional Response

Give your partner permission in your own mind to be angry with you. It's all right for him or her to be angry. It's not the end of the world, and you can handle it without becoming a mirror reflection of it. Say the words to yourself, *It's all right for (spouse's name) to be angry. I can handle it.*

*Be sure you don't reinforce or reward your spouse for becoming angry with you.* If the person yells, rants, raves and stomps around, and you respond by becoming upset or by complying with what he or she wants from you, guess what? You just reinforced your spouse's behavior. If your spouse is angry but reasonable, then respond by stating your point in a caring, logical manner. It also helps to reflect what you hear your partner saying. Let your partner know that you can understand his or her being angry and upset at this time.

*Ask your partner to respond to you in a reasonable manner.* Suggest that your spouse restate the original concern, lower his or her voice and speak to you as though you had just been introduced for the first time.

Remember: if your spouse is angry, you do not have to become angry. This may be a good time to go back and read through the Scriptures mentioned earlier. If anger interferes with the interaction between you and your spouse, there are ways you can change the pattern.

### Be Aware of Your Own Response

Identify the cues that contribute to the anger. It's important to determine how and when you express anger. What arouses it? What do you do to create the anger and keep it going? (Focus only on your part; don't lay any blame on your partner.)

One way to accomplish this is by keeping a behavior diary. Whenever anger occurs, each spouse needs to record the following:

1. The circumstances surrounding the anger, such as who was there, where it occurred, what triggered it and so on
2. The specific ways you acted and the statements you made
3. The other person's reactions to your behaviors and statements
4. The manner in which the conflict was eventually resolved (if at all)

## Interrupt the Pattern

Develop a plan of action for interrupting the conflict pattern. This plan should involve immediate action to disengage from the conflict. It also should be a way to face and handle the problem at a later time. Interrupting the conflict is an application of Nehemiah 5:6,7 (*AMP*): "I [Nehemiah] was very angry when I heard their cry and these words. I thought it over and then rebuked the nobles and officials."

The important principle to help resolve conflicts and create harmony is *delay*. When you begin to feel anger kicking open your emotional doors, delay any response. Buy time and talk yourself down by making use of the principles in this chapter. You may find it beneficial to write out some responses to use when you get angry. Practice them out loud so you can recall them when you get upset. It works.

In any expression of anger between two people, you are

responsible for your own anger, and the other person is responsible for his. You can project the anger onto your partner and hold him or her responsible for the way you feel and act, but that demands that your partner be the one to change. Holding the other person responsible is a protective response that says, "I have been victimized by you." If you focus on yourself and take responsibility for the way you feel, there's a greater chance of resolving an issue.

Instead of saying, "You made me angry," tell your spouse, "You acted in this way and *I felt* angry because of the way you behaved."

As your own anger begins to escalate, use the interruption approach on yourself. Earlier, we identified the three basic causes of anger as fear, hurt and frustration. Anger is the secondary response to any of these three emotions.

If anger is a problem for you, keep a 3x5 card with you with the word "Stop!" printed in large letters on one side. On the other side print the following three questions:

Am I experiencing hurt right now?

The important principle to help resolve conflicts and create harmony is *delay*. When you begin to feel anger kicking open your emotional doors, delay any response.

Am I afraid?

Am I frustrated over something?

The minute you begin to experience your anger rising, take out the card, read the word "Stop!" (out loud if it's appropriate) and then turn the card over. Read and respond to the three questions. Slowing down your anger response and identifying the cause will help you resolve the issue. You can still assume responsibility for choosing to respond in a way that will help defuse the other person rather than fuel the interchange.

Another positive step is to use neutral expressions such as, "I'm getting angry"; "I'm losing control"; "We're starting to fight"; or "I'm going to write out my feelings." Upon hearing one of these statements, the other person could say, "Thank you for telling me. What can I do right now that would help?"

Both of you need to make a commitment not to raise your voices or yell and not to act out your anger. It's called suspending the anger. Agree to return to the issue at a time of less conflict. Most couples are not used to taking the time to admit and scrutinize their anger and then handle it. The interruption period could be an opportune time for you to focus on the cause of your anger.

## Plan a Venting Session

Some couples have found it beneficial to schedule and structure anger ventilation sessions. Why would anyone want to plan to air their anger? Actually, a planned session will allow both individuals a greater sense of control. If the subject is so intense and the anger you feel needs to be expressed, why not be in charge of it? Some individuals have difficulty bringing up some issues unless they are angry. If a ventilation session has been planned, the couple can also exercise more control in the way the anger is expressed.

In his book *Love Is Never Enough*, Aaron Beck proposes several guidelines to make such sessions effective:

Establish a specific time and place where both can talk but not be overheard by anyone else.

Set a time limit for each session, such as 15 to 20 minutes.

Allow no interruptions, and to eliminate controlling the time, a person can talk for no more than two minutes and then must allow the other to speak.

Include, in advance, some provision for time-outs.

Avoid doing the following in any comments to your spouse: condemning the person; insulting the person; mentioning or picking on any vulnerable areas; recounting any past issues unless they pertain directly to the issue at hand; and stating that your partner made you angry. (It is far better to say, "I felt angry," than to say, "You made me angry.")[3]

The purpose of these sessions is to stay in control, to release and reduce anger and to resolve the issues. When you stay in control in this way, your spouse has the opportunity to discover the inappropriateness of his or her response and perhaps to follow your example.

## Assess Your Emotional State

Some people like to use a stress reduction card—a small square that is sensitive to heat and moisture. You place your thumb on the square for 10 seconds and your level of stress will turn the square either black, red, green or blue, depending upon how tense or excited you are. The green or blue colored zones reflect calm, with little or no stress.[4]

There are proper zones to stay in with anger as well. Beck indicates that couples often move out of the temperate (green or blue) zones of anger into the red zone. Temperate means that you are being objective and logical; red indicates intense, irrational anger. In between is what is called the yellow zone; the person feels anger toward the other person but is able to exert control over his thoughts and actions. He can still let his partner know that he is angry and needs to express it, but not at the expense of the relationship.

When a person moves from the yellow to the red zone, all the symptoms of the yellow zone have been intensified. This "red" anger is characterized by attacking the person rather than the problem, being irrational, hurling accusations, demeaning a spouse's character and believing that he or she deserves everything the angry person is dishing out. This is where lasting damage can occur. The blue zone is characterized by calm presentations and by listening.[5]

### Signal Before You Reach the Danger Zone

It is possible to learn to identify which zone you are in and let your partner know, and also to identify which zone you are working toward. As one husband said, "I'm hovering between yellow and red, and I don't like either. I want to get rid of how I'm feeling and get into the blue zone of 'please listen to me.'"

Some couples make little flags and pin them up in a predesignated spot to denote the level of their anger. (Some have made this a family project in which everyone has their own set of flags. Each person keeps his set of flags with him during a discussion or disagreement and holds the appropriate flag to let others know his or her anger level.) When a person has chosen to use the flags to convey a message about his anger, he does have some control over his emotions.

How can you keep anger from escalating in your marriage? David Viscott suggests 10 practical steps that many couples have successfully used. These guidelines can work for you, but you must be willing to implement them regardless of what your partner does. Your behavior is not dependent upon your partner's action. If it is, you've chosen to fall under his or her control. Remember, practice these steps even if your partner does not.

1. Don't wait for your feelings to accumulate. Express your hurt, fear or frustration as soon as you become aware of it.

2. Be sure to share in the language style of your partner. If your mate uses few words (a condenser) in his or her communication style, keep it brief. If he or she likes to expand and explain (an expander), offer details and sufficient information.

3. The longer you wait to express your feelings, the longer it will take to resolve them. Therefore, you decide whether you want a long discussion or a brief one. You have a choice in the matter.

4. Don't imply or even hint that your spouse has ulterior motives or isn't trustworthy. He or she will turn you off if you do.

5. Any attempts to make your partner feel guilty will come back to haunt you. Your purpose is to resolve.

6. Choose an attitude that says you will resolve the issue and there will be a positive result eventually.

7. If your partner voices attacking, personal comments, don't invest your time and energy in responding to them. Let them slide, and keep on target.

8. If you make a generalization or embellish the facts (lie a bit), stop at once and correct yourself. Use statements such as, "I'm sorry, what I really meant to say and what is more factual is . . ." Whenever you realize that your statements are not what is best, correct yourself and admit to what you have done. It's all right to say: "I was wrong in what I said"; "I was trying to get back at you because . . . "; "I admit I was trying to hurt you and I am sorry"; "I was upset at something else and I took it out on you."

9. Don't give ultimatums during your discussion. Even if one is needed, this is not the best time, and it reflects a control issue or power struggle. Ultimatums rarely work.

10. Now it's up to you to list three other guidelines that you feel would be positive and helpful. If you want this list of guidelines to work, read the list out loud every day for three weeks and you will find yourself changing.[6]

The wise King Solomon reminds us that controlling our anger makes good sense: "Good sense makes a man restrain his anger, and it is his glory to overlook a transgression or an offense" (Prov. 19:11, *AMP*).

## Living with Our Emotions

Anger will always be a part of even the healthiest of interpersonal relationships. The more intimate the relationship, the more possibility of hurt, which can lead to anger. People are afraid of anger because they fear the hurt it can bring.

Anger expressed straight-out is better than anger camouflaged. Openly sharing your anger is different than being an angry person. When expressed in a healthy, noninsulting way, anger is acceptable.

I've seen some men and women who were so uneasy with their anger that it came out as laughter—usually a nervous laugh—and then an attempt to withdraw from the other person. These people are not comfortable with their own anger and can't trust themselves enough to state in a factual way how they are feeling. Much of the time their fear of expression is the fear of conflict.

Recently, I heard someone say that more marriages today are dying from silence than from violence. Silence. Repressed feelings. Coldness. Withdrawn emotions that are still living and seething internally will do the greatest damage.

How can we know what a person is feeling or thinking if the person is frozen like an iceberg? We need to feel our anger and then reveal it. When we're in control and we express anger properly, conflicts diminish.

When hurts have accumulated in a marriage over a period of years, the anger container is usually quite full and difficult to drain. In an effort to drain the anger container, I've often asked clients to write a letter to their spouse (which will *not* be mailed) and share their feelings with that person. The letter includes not only the anger but the original feelings that generated the anger as well. I suggest that after they have written this portion of the letter, they can then write what they really want from the relationship and suggest steps to rebuild the closeness.

This last step is often the most difficult, for it involves stating that you either forgive the other person or want to come to the place of forgiving him or her. Once the letter is completed, the individual has the choice of reading it aloud at home or bringing it to my office and reading it to me. If the person reads it aloud at home, he or she goes into a room, closes the door and arranges two chairs facing each other. While sitting in one chair, the person assumes that his or her partner is in the other chair. Either process—reading the letter in my office or reading it at home—is a healthy draining of the anger container and does not antagonize the partner. The person then needs to consider what to do the next time the problem arises so that his or her anger will be in control and used in a healthy, constructive manner.

Anger is a part of life and always will be because God created us with our emotions. See your anger for what it is—a response to other feelings. And remember that you can be in control. You can change!

## Life Changers
You can control your anger if you:

1. Identify the true feeling behind your anger.
2. Apply God's Word to your anger.
3. Delay reacting to your anger!

## What's Your Plan?

1. What specific changes do you want to make in dealing with your anger?

2. Describe the plan you will implement this week to bring about these changes.

3. Go back through this chapter and list the specific points that will help you the most.

4. Describe how you would like your spouse to pray for you.

*Notes*

1. Richard P. Walters, *Anger: Yours and Mine and What to Do About It* (Grand Rapids, Mich.: Zondervan Publishing House, 1981), p. 139.

2. Carol Travis, *Anger—The Misunderstood Emotion* (New York: Simon & Schuster, 1982), pp. 220, 221, adapted.

3. Aaron T. Beck, *Love Is Never Enough* (New York: Harper & Row, 1988), pp. 272-274, adapted.

4. Ibid., pp. 270-274, adapted.

5. Ibid., pp. 274-276, adapted.

6. David Viscott, *I Love You, Let's Work It Out* (New York: Simon & Schuster, 1987), pp. 177, 178, adapted.

# THE KEY TO RESOLVING CONFLICTS

CHAPTER TWELVE

What causes fighting and quarrels among you? Is not their origin the appetites that war in your bodies? You want what you cannot have, so you murder; you are envious, and cannot attain your ambition, so you quarrel and fight. You do not get what you want, because you do not pray for it. Or, if you do, your requests are not granted, because you pray from wrong motives, in order to squander what you get on your pleasures (Jas. 4:1-3, *REB*).

These strong words were written to Christians many years ago, yet they are still applicable today. Many marriages are characterized by strife and bickering rather than peace and harmony. Couples who have developed harmony are not those who are identical in thinking, behavior and attitudes—they are not carbon copies of each other. These couples have learned to take their differences through the process of acceptance, understanding and, eventually, complementation. They have learned to speak one another's language. They have learned the uniqueness of their personalities and how to adjust to each other.

Because each person is unique and what each person brings to the marriage is unique, conflict will emerge. There will be numerous conflicts throughout the life of a marriage, and this isn't bad, it is normal. How you respond to the conflicts and deal with them are the real issues.

Let's define "conflict": Conflict . . . to strike together. 1. a fight, clash, contention. 2. sharp disagreement of opposition of interest, ideas, etc., mutual interference of incompatible forces or wills.[1]

One of the traditional ways that couples learn to deal with conflict is to suppress it—they try to forget it, sweep it under the rug or shrug it off. This so-called nice way has been equated with being Christian. Burying conflicts, however, only builds resentment that drains you of energy and colors your entire perception of daily life. When differences are buried, they are buried alive and will resurrect themselves eventually.

Some couples handle conflict by expressing their feelings unreservedly. For some this approach resembles war. Wave after wave of attack mounts and the intensity increases. In time, verbal garbage is spoken, memories are activated that would put an elephant's memory to shame, and total frustration is the end result. During this time each spouse assumes the role of a skilled lawyer, eager not only to indict the other but to see him or her convicted (and in some cases hung!).

# What Do You Think?

1. What major conflicts have you experienced in your marriage?
2. How have you managed to resolve conflicts in the past?
3. To what degree have differences in your personality and your spouse's contributed to your conflicts?

Many couples state that what pains them most about conflict is the constant quarreling. Other couples say they avoid conflict, if at all possible, because of the biblical teaching concerning quarreling. But what does the Bible say about conflict? What does it say about quarrels? Are quarreling and conflict synonymous? Not really. Many conflicts are handled and resolved without quarreling.

A quarrel has been defined as verbal strife in which angry emotions are in control, and the couple does not deal with the issue but instead each attacks the other person. The Scripture tells us not to be involved in quarrels: "Foolish people are always fighting, but avoiding quarrels will bring you honor" (Prov. 20:3, NCV). "Just as charcoal and wood keep a fire going, a quarrelsome person keeps an argument going" (Prov. 26:21, NCV). Let's consider some basic assumptions about conflict.

*Conflict is a natural phenomenon and is therefore inevitable.* Conflict arises in part because all of us perceive people and situations differently. These different perceptions allow for different opinions and choices that can cause conflict. And conflict is inevitable between people who care about each other and want to develop a deeper relationship. Dwight Small says:

The most frequent conflicts husbands and wives experience are verbal. Verbal conflict in itself is not harmful; any

Most conflict

is not dealt

with openly

because most

people have

not been

taught

effective ways

of resolving

conflict.

damage it causes depends upon the maturity of the two people in conflict. Entirely different ends can be served by a verbal clash, and some of them are healthy and good. Conflict can open doors of communication as well as shut them. As a reality in marriage, conflict can be creatively managed for good; it is part of the growth process. Don't ever underestimate its positive possibilities! . . . In a Christian marriage, conflict—with its demand for confession, forgiveness and reconciliation— is a means God employs to teach humility.[2]

*Conflict indicates a deprivation in some personal value or need.* Every human being has some very basic needs. William Glasser suggests that the most basic are the need to love and be loved and the need to feel worthwhile. Abraham Maslow describes a hierarchy of needs: We strive to fulfill our physiological needs first, then our safety needs, then our need for love and belongingness, our need for esteem and our self-actualization needs. When you have a conflict with your spouse, ask yourself which of your needs are not being met.

*Conflicts usually are as symptoms of underlying needs.* When people find themselves in conflict they usually have some need that is unfulfilled. Resolving the conflict may not solve the problem. It is better to look below the symptom to discover what need the person is striving to fulfill and resolve the need rather than the symptom only.

*Most conflict is not dealt with openly because most people have not been taught effective ways of resolving conflict.* Many couples ignore minor conflicts to keep from rocking the boat. When a major conflict arises, people tend to avoid it because they have not learned how to deal with minor conflicts. They have not developed the necessary skills by solving minor problems.

I remember the story of Fred, a landscape contractor. His first job was to remove a huge oak stump from a field. Fred had to use dynamite. The only problem was, he had never used dynamite before. He was kind of nervous about it, especially with the old farmer watching every move he made. So he tried to get the maximum effect. He didn't want to use too small an amount and have to do it over nor did he want to use too much. He went about it scientifically.

When he was ready to detonate the charge, Fred and the farmer went behind the pickup truck where a wire was running to the detonator. He looked at the farmer, said a prayer, and plunged the detonator. It worked . . . all too well. The stump broke loose from the ground, rose through the air in a curving arc and then plummeted down right on the cab of the truck. Fred's heart sank, and all he could think of was the ruined cab. Not the farmer. He was full of amazement and admiration. Slapping Fred on the back he said, "Not bad. With a little more practice you'll get it in the bed every time!"

*Conflict provides opportunity for growth in a relationship.* Conflict is like dynamite. It can be helpful if used in the right way but can also be destructive at the wrong time or in the wrong manner. Through conflict a person can share his differences with another individual. Facing conflict is also a way of testing one's strength and resources. Each person in a conflict situation will bring one or more alternative choices to the discussion. These can be explored together, and each person can learn from the other. When the conflict is resolved, there can be growth on the part of both individuals.

Again, Dr. Small states: "Disagreements come and they must be handled in one way or another. . . . We must also make the distinction that the disagreements are one thing, behaving disagreeably is quite another."[3]

*Unresolved conflicts interfere with growth and satisfying relationships.* Barriers are erected when conflicts are not resolved. We tend to become defensive in order not to be hurt. A defensive reaction places a strain on any relationship.[4]

Jesus experienced conflict. He was in constant conflict with the religious leaders of Judea. They wanted to defeat Him and get rid of Him. John 8:2-7,9-11 is an account of one of the conflicts between Jesus and the religious leaders:

And early in the morning [Jesus] came again into the temple, and all the people were coming to Him; and He sat down and began to teach them. And the scribes and the Pharisees brought a woman caught in adultery, and having set her in the midst, they said to Him, "Teacher, this woman has been caught in adultery, in the very act. Now in the Law Moses commanded us to stone such women; what then do You say?" And they were saying this, testing Him, in order that they might have grounds for accusing Him. But Jesus . . . said to them, "He who is without sin among you, let him be the first to throw a stone at her." . . . And when they heard it, they began to go out one by one, beginning with the older ones, and He was left alone, and the woman, where she had been, in the midst. . . . Jesus said to her, "Woman, where are they? Did no one condemn you?" And she said, "No one, Lord." And Jesus said, "Neither do I condemn you; go your way. From now on sin no more."

Jesus did not run or withdraw from this confrontation. Neither did He yield to the demands of the scribes and Pharisees nor did He compromise. He forced them to consider an alternative—mercy for the woman.

## Different Styles of Handling Conflict

All of us, upon entering marriage, develop a style of dealing with conflict. We might assume that our spouse will handle conflict in a similar manner, but there are many ways of handling conflict. These differences are at the heart of much of the conflict.

David and Vera Mace suggest that the conflict process looks like Diagram 1.

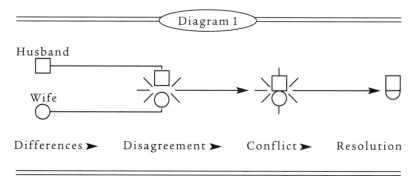

Diagram 1

Husband

Wife

Differences ➤     Disagreement ➤     Conflict ➤     Resolution

First we see the difference between husband and wife, illustrated by different shapes—a square and a circle. Next we see the difference in their wishes brought close together as a result of their desire for mutual involvement, which leads to a disagreement—each asking the other to yield.

If they continue to confront each other in a state of disagreement, frustration is stirred in both and a state of emotional heat develops. This is a conflict. They are moving into a clash of wills, a quarrel, a fight.

What they do next is critical. If they can't tolerate conflict, they will disengage and go back to where they started. The difference remains unresolved. The disagreement is recognized but avoided in the future, and the feelings of frustration suppressed. The attempt to become more deeply involved with each other, in that particular area of the relationship, is abandoned.[5]

## Withdraw

If you have a tendency to see conflict as a hopeless inevitability that you can do little to control, then you may not even bother trying. You may withdraw physically by removing yourself from the room or environment, or you may withdraw psychologically by not speaking, by ignoring the situation or by insulating yourself to such an extent that what is said or suggested has no penetrating power. Many people use the backing-off approach to protect themselves.

## Win

If your self-concept is threatened or you feel strongly that you must look after your own interests, then winning may be your choice. If you have a position of authority and it becomes threatened, winning is a counterattack. No matter what the cost, winning is the goal.

People employ many different tactics in order to win. Because married couples are well aware of each other's areas of vulnerability and hurt, they often use these areas to coerce the other person into giving in to their demands. Winners may attack self-esteem or pride in order to win. They may store up grudges and use them at the appropriate time in order to take care of a conflict. They may cash in old emotions and hurts at an opportune moment. The stockpiling approach is another form of revenge and certainly does not reflect a Christian's demonstration of forgiveness.

If winning is your style, answer the following questions:

1. Is winning necessary to build or maintain your self-esteem or to maintain a strong picture of yourself?

    People need a strong sense of self-esteem in order to find satisfaction in life and in their marriage. But what is the foundation upon which this self-esteem is built? If one is insecure or self-doubting, he often creates a false image to fool others and, in the process, confuses himself. To defer to another, to give in or to lose a debate or argument is a strong threat to the person's feelings about himself, and thus he fights to keep this from happening. The authoritarian person is not usually as secure as the image he portrays. Deferring to another is a sign of a weakening of his position.

2. Is winning necessary because you confuse wants with needs?

The spouse who feels he needs something may be more demanding about getting it than if he just wants something. Do you distinguish between needs and wants? You may see something as a need in your life but your partner may see it as a want. How do you know if something truly is a need?

## Yield

We often see yield signs on the highway; the signs are placed there for our own protection. If we yield in a conflict, we also protect ourselves. We do not want to risk a confrontation, so we give in to get along with our partner.

We all use this approach from time to time, but is yielding a regular pattern for you? Consistently yielding may create feelings of martyrdom or, eventually, guilt in your partner. We even find some individuals who need to lose in a marital conflict. Yielding is a face-saving way of doing that. By yielding, you give the appearance that you are in control and are the one behaving in the most-Christian way.

## Compromise

Another method of dealing with conflict is to compromise, or give a little to get a little. You have discovered that it's important to back off on some of your ideas or demands in order to help the other person give a little. You don't want to win all the time, nor do you want the other person to win all the time. This approach involves concessions on both sides and has been called the horse-trading technique.

## Resolve

In the resolve style of dealing with conflict, open and direct communication is used to change a situation, attitude or behavior. The couple is willing to spend sufficient time working on the difference so that even though some of their original wants and ideas have changed, they are very satisfied with the solution at which they've arrived.

Diagram 2 shows a way of diagramming the five styles of handling conflict.

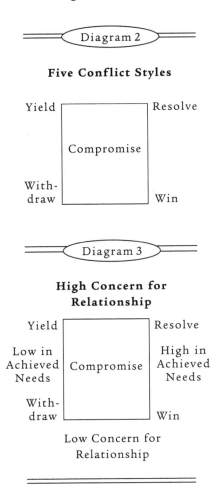

**Diagram 2**

**Five Conflict Styles**

Yield — Resolve

Compromise

Withdraw — Win

**Diagram 3**

**High Concern for Relationship**

Yield — Resolve

Low in Achieved Needs — Compromise — High in Achieved Needs

Withdraw — Win

Low Concern for Relationship

Which method of handling conflict is best or ideal? Each one has an element of effectiveness in certain situations. At times, compromise is not the best, whereas winning may be. Yielding on certain occasions can be a true and pure act of love and concern. But the ideal style we work toward is the style of resolving conflicts.

Let's look at Diagram 3.

You will notice that some new descriptive words have been added to Diagram 3. When a person uses *withdrawal* as his normal pattern of handling conflict, the relationship suffers and it is difficult to see needs being fulfilled. Withdrawal is the least-helpful style of handling conflicts. The relationship is hindered from growing and developing.

If this is your style, think about why you withdraw. It is not a demonstration of biblical submission or meekness. This method is often employed out of fear of the other person, fear of one's lack of abilities or even fear of success.

*Winning* achieves the individual's goal but at the same time sacrifices the relationship. A person might win the battle but lose the war. In a marriage, personal relationships are more important than the goal, and winning can be a hollow victory.

*Yielding* has a higher value because it appears to build the relationship, but personal goals or needs are sacrificed in yielding, which can breed resentment. Yielding may not build the relationship as much as some believe. If the relationship were that important, a person would be willing to share, confront and become assertive.

*Compromising* is an attempt to work out the relationship and attain the achievement of some needs. The bargaining involved may mean that some values are compromised. You may find that you are not satisfied with the end result, but it is better than nothing. This could actually threaten the relationship. There may be a feeling of uneasiness following the settlement.

*Resolving* conflict is the ideal toward which couples are encouraged to work. The relationship is strengthened when conflicts are resolved and needs are met on both sides. It takes longer and involves listening and acceptance, but what can be accomplished through resolution will build the relationship even more and show a greater concern for the relationship than do other methods.

When you handle conflict by resolving it, you may have changed in the process, but you're glad for the change. Because Jesus Christ is present in your life, you can give up your fears and insecurities. You can have a new boldness and new courage to confront the issues of life and, in a loving, manner, to confront others around you. Some people feel that it's impossible for them to change, but the Word of God says, "I can do all things through [Christ] who strengthens me" (Phil. 4:13).

## Truce Triggers

Sometimes conflicts seem to consume a couple's time and attention. The couple spends their energy dwelling and ruminating about their times of conflict. What makes a difference is beginning to notice what is *different* about the times the two of you are getting along. Notice what is done differently during those times compared with the times when you aren't getting along. This could be the clue you need for fewer hassles in the future.

### Concentrate on
### How Conflicts End
Often when I talk with couples about their conflicts, their attention

Often a couple's attention is on what creates the conflict. Who started it may not be as important as how and why it ended. When we discover truce triggers, we can employ them more consciously in the future.

is on what *creates* the conflict. But I like to know how the conflict *ends*. Who started it may not be as important as *how* and *why* it ends. When you can discover what are called truce triggers, you can employ these much more consciously in the future. When you shift your attention to the ending events of the conflict rather than the beginning events, you may discover why and how the conflict started.

### Identify Where Conflicts Occur

Several other steps can break the cycle of conflict in a marriage. First, identify *where* most of your conflicts occur. Is it in one location? At the dinner table? In the car? In the bedroom? Discover where conflict occurs and change the location. Make it a policy to begin your discussions in a different place.

One couple made an agreement that whenever they were moving into a conflict, they would go into the bathroom to continue it there. Usually they began to laugh, which helped them begin to resolve the issue.

### Identify When Conflicts Occur

The next step is to discover *when* the conflicts occur. Once that's been established, make an arrangement not to discuss issues at that time. Many couples have found it helpful to schedule a time to discuss issues they knew had conflict potential. Some couples even create a structure with rules, like setting a timer (you can't talk more than 30 seconds), paraphrasing aloud what you've heard your partner say (to their satisfaction) before you can talk and holding hands during the discussion.

### Identify How to Defuse Conflict

Another couple purchased two Groucho Marx-style plastic nose and glasses. Whenever they felt a conflict coming on they both put on their glasses. It consistently broke the pattern of the conflict.

Another couple developed a habit of predicting each evening whether the next day would be a good day or a bad day. At the end of the day they were to let their spouse know whether it had been a good or bad day. Because of making this prediction, the idea that they might have a good day was more of a possibility.[6]

## Steps to Conflict Resolution

You may have decided you would like to use *resolution* as your style of addressing conflict, but you're wondering what to do to bring that about. Here is a suggested format to help move you toward resolution. These suggestions will work if you spend time, make the effort and persevere. Because conflict relates to the process of communication, and because it is impossible to separate the two, many of these suggestions are basic principles of communication. They are not necessarily listed in order of importance.

*Speak directly and personally to the other person.* Don't assume the other person knows what you are thinking and feeling. If anything, assume that he or she knows very little and that this is the first time to deal with the issue. "In the end, people appreciate frankness more than flattery" (Prov. 28:23, *TLB*).

*Be honest in your statements and questions.* Ephesians 4:15,23 are important to practice, both in making statements and in asking questions. When you ask a question, does your spouse have the freedom to share an honest response? Even if you disagree with the response? If you feel that your partner has a double message behind his or her question or has an ulterior motive, respond only to the question at its face value. Don't get caught up in mind reading or second-guessing.

*Turn your questions into statements.* Too often in a conflict one or the other feels as if he or she is participating in an inquisition.

*Focus on desired expectations or positive changes* rather than on faults, defects or what you hope to avoid. This helps each of you become aware of what is gratifying and helpful to the other. Believe it or not, it's easier, psychologically speaking, to begin new behaviors than to terminate old behaviors. Don't apologize for your feelings or your needs.

When sharing what you want, *make your request in a statement of preference* rather than a statement of necessity.

When you feel unloved by your partner, *initiate loving behavior toward the person.* If you begin to perform loving acts, your spouse may act more loving toward you. But if he or she doesn't, that's all right; your act of love can fulfill some of your own needs and be a demonstration of Christ's love.

*Make "I" statements rather than "you" statements and share your present feelings* rather than your past thoughts or feelings.

*Select an appropriate time.* "A man has joy in making an apt answer, and a word spoken at the right moment—how good it is!" (Prov. 15:23, *AMP*).

*Define the problem.* How do you define the problem and how does your partner define it? You could suggest that you both stop talking and write down exactly what it is you are trying to resolve.

*Define the areas of agreement and disagreement in the conflict.* Share first with the other person what the two of you agree on, and then ask what he or she disagrees with you about. Writing the areas of agreement and disagreement on paper helps to clarify the situation.

Here comes the difficult part. *Identify your own contribution to the problem.* A few conflicts may be one-sided, but most involve contributions from both sides. When you accept some responsibility for a problem, the other person sees a willingness to cooperate and will probably be much more open to the discussion.

The next step is to *state positively what behaviors on your part would probably help; be willing to ask for his or her opinion.* As your partner shares with you, be open to his or her feelings, observations and suggestions.

## What's Your Plan?

1. Which of the five methods of dealing with conflict have you been using?
2. What will you do differently in the future to resolve conflicts in a healthier way?
3. How would you like your spouse to pray for you during the next week?

*Notes*
1. James G. T. Fairfield, *When You Don't Agree* (Scottdale, Penn.: Herald Press, 1977), p. 18.
2. Dwight Harvey Small, *After You've Said "I Do"* (Grand Rapids, Mich.: Fleming H. Revell, 1968), p. 130.
3. Ibid., p. 139.
4. Gladys Hunt, *Honey for a Child's Heart* (Elgin, Ill.: David C. Cook Publishing Co., 1977).
5. David and Vera Mace, *We Can Have Better Marriages If We Really Want Them* (Nashville, Tenn.: Abingdon Press, 1974), pp. 88-90.
6. Michele Werner-Davis, *Divorce Busting* (New York: Summit Books, 1992), pp. 1-36, 149, 150, 159, 160, adapted.

# SATISFACTION SCALE

APPENDIX

## Instructions

Answer the following 11 questions. Then fill in the Satisfaction Scale. After both of you have completed these two exercises, select a time when you can be together privately and share your responses. Covering all the items may require two or three sessions. Be sure to focus on what you want and what you can do for the future.

1. Describe how much significant time you spend together as a couple and when you spend it.

2. Describe five behaviors or tasks your partner does that you appreciate.

3. List five of your spouse's personal qualities that you appreciate.

4. How frequently do you affirm or reinforce your spouse for the behaviors and qualities described in numbers 2 and 3?

5. List four important requests you ask of your spouse. How frequently do you make these requests? What is your spouse's response?

6. List four important requests your spouse asks of you. How frequently does he or she make these requests? What is your response?

7. What do you appreciate most about your spouse's communication?

8. How do you let your spouse know that you love him or her?

9. How does your spouse let you know that he or she loves you?

10. What has been one of the most fulfilling experiences in your marriage?

11. What personal and marital behaviors would you like to change in yourself?

## Satisfaction Scale

### Instructions

Use an X to indicate your level of satisfaction in each element of your relationship listed below.  0 = no satisfaction; 5 = average; 10 = super, fantastic, the best.

Use a circle to indicate what you think your partner's level of satisfaction is at the present time.

1.  Our daily personal involvement with each other

    0   1   2   3   4   5   6   7   8   9   10

2.  Our affectionate, romantic interaction

    0   1   2   3   4   5   6   7   8   9   10

3.  Our sexual relationship

    0   1   2   3   4   5   6   7   8   9   10

4.  The frequency of our sexual contact

    0   1   2   3   4   5   6   7   8   9   10

5.  My trust in my spouse

    0   1   2   3   4   5   6   7   8   9   10

6.  My spouse's trust in me

    0   1   2   3   4   5   6   7   8   9   10

7.  The depth of our communication together

    0   1   2   3   4   5   6   7   8   9   10

8.  How well we speak one another's language

    0   1   2   3   4   5   6   7   8   9   10

9. The way we divide chores

0   1   2   3   4   5   6   7   8   9   10

10. The way we make decisions

0   1   2   3   4   5   6   7   8   9   10

11. The way we manage conflict

0   1   2   3   4   5   6   7   8   9   10

12. Adjustment to one another's differences

0   1   2   3   4   5   6   7   8   9   10

13. Amount of free time together

0   1   2   3   4   5   6   7   8   9   10

14. Quality of free time together

0   1   2   3   4   5   6   7   8   9   10

15. Amount of free time apart

0   1   2   3   4   5   6   7   8   9   10

16. Our interaction with friends as a couple

0   1   2   3   4   5   6   7   8   9   10

17.   The way we support each other in rough times

0   1   2   3   4   5   6   7   8   9   10

18.   Our spiritual interaction

0   1   2   3   4   5   6   7   8   9   10

19.   Our church involvement

0   1   2   3   4   5   6   7   8   9   10

20.   The level of our financial security

0   1   2   3   4   5   6   7   8   9   10

21.   How we manage money

0   1   2   3   4   5   6   7   8   9   10

22.   My spouse's relationship with my relatives

0   1   2   3   4   5   6   7   8   9   10

23.   My relationship with my spouse's relatives

0   1   2   3   4   5   6   7   8   9   10

Select any three areas that have a score of 3 or less, and indicate what needs to occur for you to have a higher level of satisfaction in this area. Also discuss how you have tried to work on this issue.

# Best-Sellers
# from Regal

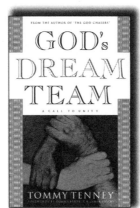
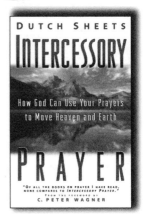

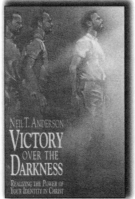
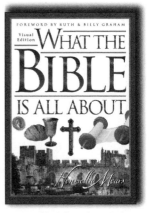